Toyota's Improvement Thinking from the Inside

This book helps close the gap in how organizations think about and implement Toyota's continuous improvement methods and management system. The Toyota Production System (TPS) is often viewed and adopted in organizations as a collection of tools to remove waste and streamline processes to provide products or services faster, better, or cheaper. While the tools for improvement and management routines are important, they are not where the true power of the system lies. The author's eight-year journey inside Toyota was full of experiences that developed the power for continuous improvement. These learnings are rarely if ever captured in books on lean or taught in business and engineering classrooms.

This book describes, in part, how Toyota, through its coaches and leaders, develops its members' capabilities through a series of continuous improvement (kaizen and problem-solving) activities. For many members of Toyota, this process results in a personal transformation that ultimately leads to organizational transformation.

This book presents a model for organizational transformation that includes technical systems, organizational principles/values, and spirituality/mindset to achieve enduring high performance. This book shifts from the continuous improvement development way at Toyota to case studies illustrating the thinking and mindset to other organizations on their journey to transformation. It uses the TPS tools as an entry point for development and highlights the role that organizational values play in the pace of transformation. Several case studies are presented that include manufacturing (performance improvement of a production line), healthcare (improvement in neurosurgery patient flow), and education (improvement in standardized test scores).

The key benefit of this book is that it provides insights into Toyota's culture and improvement thinking to help other organizations reach enduring high performance. The book is written for a wide audience so that readers outside of manufacturing organizations can understand the broad

applicability of the Toyota way. In addition, it is written succinctly to help readers and practitioners focus their transformation efforts.

Sarah K. Womack is a distinguished researcher and consultant in the field of Industrial Engineering. Her Ph.D. in the department of Industrial & Operations Engineering from the University of Michigan, Ann Arbor focused on the intersection of lean manufacturing practices and ergonomics. She has published peer-reviewed articles, presented as guest speaker at conferences and universities, and facilitated copious workshops on lean manufacturing. She has established herself as a leading scholar and consultant of one of the world's most coveted management systems, the Toyota Production System. She spent eight years on a journey in various leadership roles of "learning by doing" under some of the world's greatest lean thinkers at Toyota. Applying Toyota's management thinking, she consults across an array of industries with an innovative and practical approach to continuous improvement, organizational transformation, and operational excellence - coaching at every level from the C-suite to the shopfloor. She continues to learn and collect a patchwork of stories to teach and inspire others on their operational excellence journeys. In addition to her writing, consulting, and speaking engagements, Sarah is passionate about traveling the world and immersing herself in diverse cultures.

Toyota's Improvement Thinking from the Inside

From Personal Transformation to Organizational Transformation

Sarah K. Womack

A PRODUCTIVITY PRESS BOOK

First published 2025
by Routledge
605 Third Avenue, New York, NY 10158

and by Routledge
4 Park Square, Milton Park, Abingdon, Oxon, OX14 4RN

Routledge is an imprint of the Taylor & Francis Group, an informa business

© 2025 Sarah K. Womack

The right of Sarah K. Womack to be identified as author of this work has been asserted by them in accordance with sections 77 and 78 of the Copyright, Designs and Patents Act 1988.

All rights reserved. No part of this book may be reprinted or reproduced or utilised in any form or by any electronic, mechanical, or other means, now known or hereafter invented, including photocopying and recording, or in any information storage or retrieval system, without permission in writing from the publishers.

Trademark notice: Product or corporate names may be trademarks or registered trademarks, and are used only for identification and explanation without intent to infringe.

ISBN: 9781032889870 (hbk)
ISBN: 9781032881157 (pbk)
ISBN: 9781003540670 (ebk)

DOI: 10.4324/9781003540670

Typeset in Garamond
by Deanta Global Publishing Services, Chennai, India

To Liz, DJ, Sam, and Rocky

Contents

Foreword x

Preface xiii

Acknowledgments xvi

1 The TPS Way to Personal and Organizational Transformation ...1
Onboarding Part 1 – Standardized Work Kaizen Training 2
Onboarding Part 2 – Two Weeks on the Production Line 7
   TWI Training Way and Team Leader 8
   Team Relations 10
   My Body 10
Onboarding Part 3 – Standardized Work "Try on Own" 11
The Change Point: Double Consciousness and Values 14
The Transformation Model 16
Sharing the Good News 19

2 Technical Systems, Values, and a Culture of Improvement 21
Stability and Muda 23
Jidoka – Integrating Respect, Quality, and Productivity 23
Just-in-Time 25
Continuous Flow and Takt Time 25
Pull System (like a Supermarket) 26
Heijunka 27
Standardization 28
Safety and Safe Process Design in Transformation 28
   Ergonomics in Daily Management 29
Kaizen 29
Problem-Solving 30

vii

viii ■ *Contents*

Culture and Transformational Values 33
  Work Setting 34
  Organization Structure and Ways 35
  Improvement 37
  Discipline 38
  Teamwork 38
  Communication 39
Culture and the Transformation Model 40

3 Problem-Solving – Oh the Places You'll Go 42
Paint Shop Overview 43
Problem-Solving in Jishuken 44
  Step 1: Clarify the Problem 46
  Step 2: Break Down the Problem 47
  Step 3: Target Setting 53
  Step 4: Root Cause Analysis 54
  Steps 5 and 6: Develop and Implement Countermeasures 56
  Steps 7 and 8: Monitor the Results/Processes and Standardize 58
Storytelling and Report-Out 59
Conclusion 59

4 Continuous Improvement (CI) Implementation in Other
Organizations (Manufacturing) 62
Creation of a Continuous Improvement Model 63
Production Control Will Level (Heijunka) Incoming Customer Orders 66
Pull System to Manage Production and Stores 67
Processes and Conveyance Have Standardized Work 68
Daily Management and Living the Values 68
From Ideal to Just-Do-It 69
Problem-Solving 72
Results 73
Reflections 73

5 CI Implementation in Healthcare and Education 76
Contemporary View of Improvement in Healthcare 77
Traditional Hospital Culture and the Transformational Values 78
Clarify the Business/Customer Need 80
Grasp the Initial Condition 81
Ideal Condition and Plan 83
Just-Do-It and Results 85

Reflections 86
   Standardization...87
CI Implementation in Education...87
A Framework for Quality Improvement in Education.............................88
Continuous Improvement Thinking Applied in K–12 Education............90
   Clarify the Gap...91
   Break Down the Problem..92
   Target Setting and Root Cause..94
   Countermeasure 94
   Results...95
Yokoten (Spread) the Results...96

Conclusion **101**

Appendix **103**

References **113**

Index **115**

Foreword

I first came across TSSC, at that time the Toyota Supplier Support Center, after spending some years studying Toyota's management system including the Toyota Production System (TPS). I had the opportunity to work with some former Toyota managers from their Georgetown, Kentucky plant as a consultant to Ford. Ford was developing the Ford Production System, based on the Toyota Production System, which had been based on the original Ford Production System. I learned a lot but wanted to find out how Toyota did it when working with outside companies.

TSSC was set up to teach TPS in American, non-Toyota companies, by developing "model lines." They would work with internal people to transform an operation or value stream in one part of the plant to follow all the TPS concepts. I approached TSSC about studying their processes, which never got approved, but they did entertain me for one day in Kentucky. I visited first a traditional manufacturing facility that they had not worked with and saw waste everyplace. It was chaotic. Then I visited a kind of failure where they had successfully developed a one-piece flow work cell, which was humming, and it sat as an island within a sea of wasteful manufacturing centers. The industrial engineer in charge did not like TPS and had no interest in spreading the practices even though they performed at several times the existing level of productivity and quality. Finally, I visited what became a showcase company for TSSC called Summit Polymers. They made plastic heat and air conditioning registers on the dashboard. I later visited their Michigan operations and saw traditional batch processes without flow and with waste everywhere. What I saw in Kentucky was simple, yet, an engineering marvel in the flow of material from door to door without interruption and little visible waste anyplace. There was also evidence that team members working in production were solving problems as they occurred. In that day my paradigm about what TPS was flipped. I felt a new awareness of what manufacturing, in fact, any process to serve customers could be like.

When Sarah Womack, one of my PhD students, told me she had an offer to work in Toyota in their internal group that taught TPS I was excited, and frankly a bit envious. I had never heard of an outsider going directly into that group, let alone a PhD. She had done a unique dissertation combining ergonomics under a professor who co-chaired the committee with me, and TPS. She did case studies of an American manufacturer compared to Toyota and studied the plants looking at them from both TPS and ergonomics perspectives. But she had no practical experience with TPS. I was pretty sure her experience at Toyota, particularly this special part of Toyota, would be a cultural awakening for Sarah and she would learn a whole new deeper way of thinking about TPS. And as I read this book Sarah wrote I was right.

There is something very different about the way TPS experts within Toyota approach organizational transformation. It is thoughtful, respectful, and deeper than anything I have experienced outside of Toyota. Outsiders, such as Americans who work for Toyota, go through a personal transformation in a way that is hard to describe. Yet, Sarah does a marvelous job describing her personal transformation and how that can be scaled to an organizational level though her own journey and what she experienced working with other organizations in manufacturing and service, for profit and not-for profit.

I love the three-legged stool model Sarah developed to explain TPS—Technical Tools, Organizational Values/Principles and Spirituality/Mindset. Before discussing this book with Sarah the third leg—Spirituality/Mindset—would not have occurred to me. It has been clear in all my work that TPS is a system, and it is more than tools. One way of looking at it is as a sociotechnical system in which the social side works in harmony with the technical side. But even this seems rather clinical and mechanistic. There is something more. As Sarah explains it is about "the higher purpose of the organization." Many people analyzing Toyota talk about something called a mindset, but it is often difficult to describe. I agree with Sarah that it is about a sense of purpose that can only be explained through the concept of spirituality. It is more than a material exchange relationship with the organization—a fair day's pay for a fair day's work. For many it becomes a calling as evidenced by the many high-achieving managers and executives within Toyota who could make several times their salaries by leaving and joining another company. Yet, they stay. They feel something special working for Toyota.

We are fortunate to have this book to learn about "Toyota's Improvement Thinking from the Inside." It is one thing to have lived it and something entirely different to be able to capture in words the journey, the feeling, and the essence. Somehow Sarah has managed to do this and give you that insider's view and feel. It is very different from sterile courses on lean six-sigma management. It is in many ways the essence of humanity striving toward perfection, yet realizing it is always out of reach.

Make a few notes before you read this book about what you think lean, or learning organization, or high-performance organization is. Then compare that to your understanding after reading this book. I predict a paradigm shift as I experienced visiting TSSC learning sites. Then try to apply what you learn. For example, try the exercise Sarah had to go through of studying some process and coming up with 30 improvement ideas. It is a struggle, and without struggle there is no learning.

Jeffrey K. Liker
Author of *The Toyota Way* and Professor Emeritus,
Industrial and Operations Engineering, University of Michigan

Preface

As a doctoral student at the University of Michigan in the Department of Industrial and Operations Engineering, I was lucky enough to study under co-advisors Dr. Thomas Armstrong and Dr. Jeffrey Liker. Tom was a highly regarded researcher in the field of ergonomics, and Jeff was highly regarded in the field of engineering management and specifically lean manufacturing. Both had conducted a considerable amount of research in various manufacturing organizations, including the Big 3 automotive companies who all conducted business and operations in the Detroit, MI area.

At that time, there had been growing research and evidence that lean manufacturing practices were "mean" and leading to, or at the very least, linked to higher rates of poor health and safety outcomes in the U.S. and abroad. Intrigued by the drama of the conflict and funded by various sources, I examined the intersection of these two fields answering questions such as how can we operationalize and measure the social constructs of lean practices and more importantly find casual links to worker health? I was fortunate to be in that intersection because I would eventually need and use both specializations in my professional practice.

The University of Michigan would also host an annual lean manufacturing conference, open to the public, and bring in presenters who were heavyweights in lean research and practice such as James Womack and John Shook. The idea was to keep the network, dialogue, research, and information sharing going and growing, which was important because by many accounts, it was difficult for American (and Western thinking) organizations to effectively implement Toyota's brand of lean manufacturing and best practices. In fact, when Jeff had published *The Toyota Way* (2004) – which became a NY Times best-seller - it was extremely helpful to have more insight into the exemplar organization for all things quality, productivity, profitability, and whose production system was branded as "lean."

xiv ■ *Preface*

This was the start of my journey of understanding the gap between lean organization theory and practice, and I would learn why. After completing my doctoral studies, I started a full-time position at Toyota Engineering & Manufacturing North America (TEMA), the company's North American headquarter for engineering and manufacturing operations. I hired into the Operations Management and Development Division (OMDD), whose primary role was to develop Toyota Production System (TPS) thinking and leadership capability across Toyota's fourteen manufacturing sites in the US, Canada, and Mexico. I entered as a specialist (non-management) in OMDD. They say learning requires sacrifice, which was true in this case as my starting salary was comparable to what I earned prior to graduate school. (Note: it would pay off not only in learning, but I married a Toyota team member with whom I had three amazing children.)

To be clear, it wasn't typical for TEMA, especially OMDD, to hire someone with a PhD. It just so happened that a colleague I had met from Toyota years earlier had a job opening in his division and encouraged me to apply just as I hit the job market. The timing of it felt divine and since they were considered the best in lean manufacturing, I applied and was offered a position in the group. I am certain there was some reservation on their part because there was no prestige associated with the position - they simply wanted someone willing to be developed and was eager to learn.

My academic and research background in lean manufacturing was helpful, but nothing prepared me for the culture shock I would experience. I recall speaking to Jeff Liker about my onboarding experience while he was publishing *Toyota Way to Continuous Improvement* (2011), and he succinctly captured the matter in his signing of that book in Figure 0.1.

> My eight-year journey inside of Toyota in several roles, traveling throughout North America and Japan, working with leaders and team members within the company, suppliers and organizations outside of manufacturing, was full of experiences that unequivocally transformed my way of thinking. Like a rock under pressure that produces a diamond so too was how I (and other members) developed a deeper understanding of the real Toyota Way and true TPS to become a new kind of thinker and practitioner in the field of lean/operational performance/operational excellence.

While the idea and philosophy of continuous improvement with all its goodness and hope is as old as religion, these experiences are rarely if ever

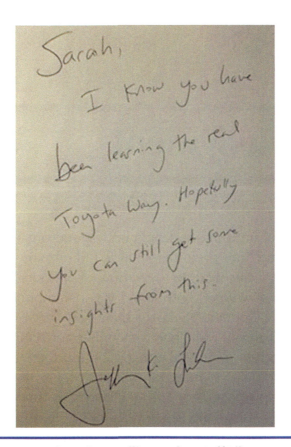

Figure 0.1 Note from NY Times best-selling author, Jeff Liker

captured in books on lean or taught in business and engineering classrooms. A plethora of college courses and professional trainings are offered on modern continuous improvement practice including six sigma, lean, lean-six sigma, etc., but none of these compare to the depth of knowledge and wisdom that engulfs continuous improvement at Toyota, which I hope is clearly communicated in this book.

Acknowledgments

The journey I set out on to more deeply understand organizational continuous improvement and high performance was full of many helpful people from the University of Michigan to the various shopfloors and beyond. There were some individuals whose contribution was paramount including Bryant Sanders and Toyota's Operations Management and Development Division, Hideshi Yokoi and Toyota Production System Support Center, Inc., Jim Boss, Melody Siska, Smriti Neogi, Emily Durban, and Elizabeth Simms.

Writing this book was a journey in itself and would not have been possible without the helpful hands of Jeffrey Liker, John Shook, Katrina Appell, Regina Whitfield-Kekessi, Diane Bradley, Laura Ulrich, Chet Marchwinski, Jacob Stoller, Lynn Kelley, Tracey Richardson, and Michael Sinocchi.

Chapter 1

The TPS Way to Personal and Organizational Transformation

Toyota and specifically the Toyota Production System (TPS) have become a global model for best practice in what is often referred to as a lean enterprise, learning organization, high-reliability organization, total quality management system, lean-six sigma, and so on. TPS is often viewed and adopted in organizations as a collection of tools used to remove the waste and non-value-added things that people do and streamline processes to get products or services delivered faster, better, or at a lower cost. However, merely studying lean tools and methodologies from books and lectures can at best be only the beginning of the journey and at worst lead to people and organizations going in the wrong direction.

My own study of lean manufacturing in many ways did not prepare me for Toyota's culture, more specifically the Operations Management and Development Division (OMDD) culture. In many ways, it felt like training for a military special forces unit of highly effective members who get deployed to various manufacturing facilities to quickly grasp the condition of shop-floor operations, establish and execute a kaizen (improvement) plan, and develop the local management in the process. The pace was fast, the work demands were high (sometimes seemingly impossible), learning was deep and happened by trial and error (not over-analyzing and making assumptions from a computer or desk), and the social rules for engagement were rigid – all of which necessitated coaching.

DOI: 10.4324/9781003540670-1

Onboarding Part 1 – Standardized Work Kaizen Training

My first onboarding activity was a standardized work kaizen training activity – the basic training or boot camp for preparation in the war against muda (or non-value-added work, also called waste). In TPS, most (if not all) repetitive production processes are standardized, meaning they have specifically described steps to ensure efficiency, safety, timing, and quality. Standardized work kaizen is not only defined uniquely in TPS but also conducted in a very specific and disciplined manner to discover improvements in the layout, tools and equipment, materials, and movements of the team member(s) performing the process.

My first week in the office I was headed to Toyota's engine production facility in West Virginia for a 3.5-day standardized work kaizen training. I traveled by car with an OMDD assistant manager and used the drive time to inquire about his experiences and thoughts about working at Toyota. His responses seemed very measured and careful, as if he were holding back in his responses. Nevertheless, he was full of stories, the most memorable of which was when he accompanied a Toyota Japanese executive on a trip to visit an (American) supplier. He said the Japanese executive abruptly walked out of the meeting and sat in the car waiting for his team to rejoin because the American executives were not interested in going to the shop-floor to discuss their actual condition and instead insisted on delivering their PowerPoint presentation from the office. I was full of intrigue.

Once we arrived at the engine production facility, we hit the ground running, sometimes literally. We set up camp in a conference room, a 5-minute walk from our activity area. There were six trainees (including myself) participating from various organizations including OMDD and the engine facility. There were three OMDD assistant managers, all American, who facilitated and coached us through the activity. We were told (in a briefing for the mission) that their engine production facility needed to reduce the gap in productivity between actual labor and management's projected labor. On reconnaissance for this mission, the coaches and shop manager had pre-determined the area of the kaizen activity through nemawashi (the iterative process of communicating and getting approval), getting input from key stakeholders, and revising a plan to arrive at final approval. The shop leader also informed the production and maintenance members of the activity and established any necessary quality control procedures to confirm our activity did not disrupt quality. They chose an engine subassembly line with seven processes and production team members that was conveyor paced to

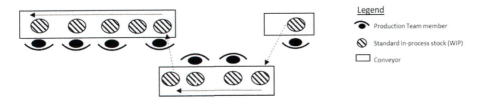

Figure 1.1 Top-view seven-process subassembly line

produce one unit every 55 seconds. Figure 1.1 shows the top-view layout of the processes and flow of material (with pointed arrows). They divvied the seven processes among the six trainees.

The coaches made sure to keep all trainees on pace given the amount of work required to accomplish the mission in 3.5 days – even if that meant staying late into the evening to help a trainee. The schedule overview included one day of capturing the initial condition of the processes and identifying muda and problems using Toyota's internally created standardized work documentation tools. On the second day, coaches guided us through creating a line balancing charts and graphics, setting a new target for the number of processes, and conducting kaizen trials to test our improvement ideas. The third day was a continuation of kaizen trials and creation of the new standardized work documents after all kaizens were completed. The final half-day was preparing the group to report out to OMDD's and the engine facility's management. The coaches also facilitated morning and afternoon meetings with the group to provide general information, receive updates on progress, and give group feedback. Within the fixed daily schedule, trainees were given considerable autonomy to work so the coaches also periodically sought out each trainee to provide support.

In addition to activity coordination and technical skill development, the coaches were the cultural gatekeepers – determining what behaviors were acceptable and unacceptable for the trainees. For example, some trainees were scolded by the coaches for having their hands in their pockets on the shopfloor. Some trainees were scolded for having their arms crossed while observing the process. Sitting was not permitted unless it was back at our training room (aka base camp). Most trainees interpreted this coaching style as militaristic, almost cult-like. I would later learn that there was some basic thinking around the behaviors that were typically transferred to American managers from TMC Japan members who apparently were concerned about the risk of team members falling (so they believed it was safer to have no hands in pockets) and showing respect (with your body) to production team members when observing their process. The training was also designed to feel competitive based on the condensed schedule, which automatically created a sense of urgency, each trainee focused mainly on their assigned process (not helping each other), and the coaches were intentionally vague with providing direction and information to trainees.

On this first day of the kaizen activity, we spent a better part of the 13-hour workday at the subassembly line capturing the initial condition of our assigned processes using stopwatches, clip boards, and cameras – and documenting and analyzing what we observed on the Toyota's standardized work kaizen tools: time measurement sheet, standardized work combination table, standardized work chart, machine capacity sheet, and work balance chart. Figures A.1–A.8 in the appendix provide a brief overview of this quintessential way of analyzing and improving work. I was familiar with these tools as they were rooted in scientific management and work measurement used in traditional industrial engineering practice to help determine a fair day's work (Taylor, 1911, 1998; Niebel & Freivalds, 2003) and improvement of safety and efficiency (Gilbreth, 1911; Barnes, 1980). Toyota adapted these work measurement methods to fit its needs and philosophical view around standardization and kaizen (Rother & Harris, 2001; Liker & Meier, 2006).

One of the most profound experiences that pointed to Toyota's obsession with data/facts was the level of scrutiny with which the coaches examined our documents – verifying the calculations and emphasizing fractions of a second savings, questioning how clearly the data showed the problems and logically connected to a proposed target (condition). I bumped heads with a coach because I was not used to or prepared for that level of minutia or style of coaching. When a coach asked a question about our process or documentation, the best response was one based on the facts. It was also okay to admit that you were unsure, then go back to the gemba (Japanese term for where the value-added work is performed) and verify the facts. The unacceptable response was one based on assumptions, often met with subtle forms of humiliation in front of the group. A coach once asked a trainee upon examination of the trainee's documents how he knew the line speed was 55 seconds. The trainee responded, "That's what I was told." The coach in silence gave the trainee a condescending gaze and slight lateral neck bend, to which the quick-witted trainee responded, "I should go measure it to make sure."

For the most part, the teaching style of the coaches was Socratic – answering trainees' questions with counter-questions to force the trainee to think more deeply and inquiring of trainees why they chose certain directions over others. The exception I noticed was when a trainee was not familiar with the TPS tools or concepts, the coaches would then give clearer direction. For the rest of the group, the coaches were intentionally vague and the Socratic method only worked top-down, not bottom-up. For example, I once inquired of a coach the theoretical basis for a sample size of 10 on the time measurement sheet when the popular rule of thumb for data collection was 30, or it otherwise could be calculated statistically (Niebel & Freivalds, 2003, see appendix). To this question, I did not get a direct answer, and coaches had enough influence to easily redirect the conversation. At that point in my TPS journey, I didn't know if this was some sort of jealousy of and retaliation against my academic background or something else. So, I simply compartmentalized it and moved on.

After capturing the initial condition of our processes and documenting it on the standardized work analysis tools, we were challenged to identify and kaizen at least 30 occurrences of muda in our process, regardless of how big or small. The initial condition of my process was fairly stable with efficient placement of parts, so it was a struggle for me to come up with 30 ideas for kaizen. My starting point was to look at how well the job was designed using principles of the motion economy, efficient movement of the hands and body (Gilbreth, 1911). Were bolts presented one by one or jumbled in a bin? Were parts designed to have clear sensory feedback such as a click or visual indicator when properly engaged to reduce the amount of force used? Were poka-yoke devices used to force selection of the correct part? Was the location of parts and tools close to their point of use? Were team members' left and right hands used simultaneously to perform tasks? Identifying muda outside of these principles required me (and the other trainees) to think more outside of the box. Personally, when I struggle to find a solution or think outside of the box, I have to (mentally) distance myself from the noise of the environment, meditate on the goal and purpose, pray for clarity, and wait for the revelation, which seems to always come on time. This way plus support from the coaches was effective and got me through that (and most) challenges in the training.

After identifying muda, each trainee set individual kaizen targets for their process. I aimed to reduce my process's cycle time by 7 seconds and the fluctuation by 8 seconds. Fluctuation (defined as the difference between the highest and lowest observed cycle times) was an interesting metric to kaizen because the causes of fluctuation seemed random and could vary considerably between cycles for the same team member and certainly between team members. Some examples of causes of fluctuation are dropping a bolt, adjusting parts to fit properly, selecting the wrong part from a bin, starting the next work cycle too early or late, etc. After thinking about fluctuation more deeply, I could see how it was useful for further improving the stability of a process (which ultimately impacted productivity), and more importantly, it shifted our attention and kaizen focus on each team member's burden.

Before making any changes on a process, we made the production team members aware that we planned to run kaizen trials in order to measure the improvement impact and determine if the result was "OK" or "no-good". Speediness of trials was key as there was only one full day of kaizen trials, and innovation, creativity, and speed were key attributes in this training. There was no budget for kaizen supplies, so for some countermeasures we had to forage through the facility for cardboard, duct-tape, plastic tubing, etc. to quickly mock up a trial. The coaches and production team members had ideas to help guide our kaizen efforts. What made the Socratic style of the coaches somewhat palatable was their helpfulness on and insights into how to quickly mock up and test a kaizen, working side by side with us – this also established some sense of teamwork and unity in a largely competitive hunger-games-like training framework. For some kaizen trials, we had to wait for maintenance members who at times were busy with production problems. Maintenance team members, often the superstars of the kaizen effort, were heavily relied upon to quickly make tooling and equipment layout changes, move electrical and pneumatic lines for the power tools, and often do so between shifts when production was not running. The production team members were incredibly valuable for identifying problems not easily seen, often sharing the history of problems and countermeasures with the process, and graciously participating in our kaizen trials, which required mentally balancing the current and newly proposed methods while also ensuring their quality. The collaboration between the kaizen team, maintenance members, and production team members while new and strange to me seemed banal from the shopfloor perspective, as if being watched and disrupted for the sake of kaizen was normal.

From the individual kaizen targets set by each trainee, the coaches challenged us to reduce the number of processes from seven to six. By the end of the kaizen trials, the kaizen training team met the manpower goal and the engine subassembly line indeed ran with six processes, a 14.3% productivity improvement, and created the new standardized work documents. Each trainee summarized the key aspects of his/her activities and the results and presented them at a final report-out on the shopfloor to OMDD's and the engine facility's management. Their reporting way was also very specific, requiring considerable feedback from the OMDD coaches to get each trainee's presentation to an acceptable level of storytelling using mock-ups, photos, and the standardized work documents. The storytelling also included a detail of what each member learned in reflection of the activity (most trainees spoke of the technical learning because it felt safe). After the report-out, the shop's management thanked us for our hard work, and they were left to internally review the changes and complete any open items.

The mission was complete, and we drove back to TEMA after the report-out. I was physically and mentally exhausted from the long days, fast pace, and strange coaching way, but I felt energized that the mission was successful from a performance improvement perspective. Since I was already familiar with the standardized work tools, my biggest learning from the training was an insight into TPS culture. This was my initiation into TPS and way finding – the moment I began to realize that I was different from the more experienced Toyota members and that my TPS knowledge gained outside of the company was insufficient.

Taiichi Ohno, considered to be the father of TPS, in his book on the *Toyota Production System* hinted toward this cultural way as management by ninjutsu – acquiring management skills through intense training as in the way of the ninja (Ohno, 1988). Steven Spear in a *Harvard Review* article also details an executive's TPS onboarding experience with similar themes (Spear, 2004). TPS members, regardless of management level and role, were expected to develop their kaizen mind and these cultural ways of knowing and behaving that lie beneath the technical tools for improvement. These ways resulted in a landscape of negative emotions not typically experienced during onboarding, but had to be managed as the TPS coaches were primarily responsible for members' development, not member's feelings. And good coaches were also the key to breaking the bad habits that block the good thinking required for improvement work.

Onboarding Part 2 – Two Weeks on the Production Line

Soon after the standardized work kaizen training, I was off to my next training assignment at Toyota Motor Manufacturing, Kentucky (TMMK), a vehicle and engine assembly facility in Georgetown, Kentucky, to work on the assembly line as a production team member. How very excited I was to immerse myself in the world of production – vastly different from the still, empty, and quiet office space at TEMA. Also, I was keenly interested in the design and assembly of vehicles – an incredibly complex engineering product. This would also be an opportunity to show those who perceived me as purely academic that I had some "street credibility" – this term was actually used by a manager. My manager had coordinated with TMMK's management to set up the logistics for my two-week assignment on the production line.

When I arrived at TMMK, one thing that stood out was how incredibly busy was the shopfloor – production and conveyance team members, team leaders, maintenance, management, engineering, and support personnel – everyone seemed to have full work. I started with a standard two-day classroom training for assembly production workers, learning concepts such as how to ergonomically hold power tools, pick up bolts efficiently, quality check for critical safety components (e.g., seat belt bolts), quality check the stability of electrical connectors using a push-pull-push motion, etc. The TMMK assembly shop manager had chosen for me a process on the first Trim production line, installing the engine's main wire (EMW process), which ran at one vehicle every 60 seconds. The main wire was a bundle of wires and terminals that controlled the vehicle's electrical systems such as the lights, alternator, battery, fuel injectors, fuses, etc. and sits in the engine compartment (under the hood). I was excited to learn yet baffled that I would get such an important component given my limited experience in production. I arrived at the Trim line on a Monday at the start of the first shift, 6:30 am, and was introduced to the Trim 1 team members as a trainee from OMDD. There were about 20 people (and processes) on the Trim 1 line, whose tenure ranged from 2 to 18 years with the company. The team, especially downstream processes, was reminded to look over my work to check for quality. Additionally, until I passed a competency evaluation for the EMW process, my work should have been 100% inspected by my trainer or an experienced team member who stood in my work pitch (the walking and work area).

TWI Training Way and Team Leader

The gold standard for production training at TMMK was based on Training Within Industry (TWI) job instruction methods (Donald Dinero, 2005, Productivity Press). TWI was developed in the United States during World War II to train a new and diverse workforce in industry and to ensure quality and safety. The job instruction method calls for the trainer to break the job (or process) into discrete and sequential steps, explaining each step while performing it. The trainer repeats the steps several times while performing it, adding key safety, quality, and/or productivity key points and the reasons for those key points. This redundant and progressive way was effective especially for information retention. In addition to the TWI training methods, the TMMK Assembly training standard was to become proficient in the process within two weeks, progressing in increments of 25% of the work content.

The TWI training way was more ideal than actual for my EMW process training. The team leader explained the layout and parts for the process and the 60 cycles, broken down into discrete work steps (without any key points). It wasn't long into my training before my team leader was pulled away to handle a production problem and I was left to observe the normal production team member on the process – three of whom rotated quarterly for each shift, but others also knew the process. I noticed team members performing the work steps in slightly different ways based on what was easiest for them (a point I will clarify in later discussions of standardized work). The noise level in the area was high enough to require hearing protection, and it took time for me to audibly adjust to have conversations without removing my ear buds. For the first few days, I mostly observed and tried to hold my questions until breaks or unscheduled downtime.

While training, I basically learned at my own pace, fully supported by the normal production team member who stepped in to complete the work cycle until I could keep pace. Even though the assembly training standard was two weeks, after five days I was able to perform the process 100% on my own. It helped I studied a copy of the standardized work documents. The team leader verified my proficiency, and subsequently, I was performing the process and confirming my own quality without any support. My quality and timing were decent even though I once forgot to set one of a dozen clips, a defect caught a few processes downstream. My team leader immediately made me aware of the issue. While I felt awful for the less-than-perfect quality, it felt good to know that team members were verifying quality beyond their own.

Working and training in a production setting increased my empathy for the team leader role – one of the busiest roles in the facility with many upward demands from production team members and downward demands from group leaders. The team leader position is not management and pays only slightly more than a regular production member position. They are responsible for training, responding to team members' calls for help on the line (which happened continuously throughout the shift depending on incoming quality, worker experience, etc.), filling in for missing team members, performing quality checks, following up safety/ergonomic or quality concerns, auditing standardized work for team members, and more. Some people are attracted to the position because it is a necessary first step for

10 ■ *Toyota's Improvement Thinking from the Inside*

those seeking to advance into management. Others prefer it over the monotony of working the same two to four production processes every day.

Team Relations

Once I felt comfortable with the process, I really sunk into the work, the people, and work life. I started noticing the banter, sport team rivalries, the gossip, the silence, the bible studies, card games, and other break activities, which breathed life into the otherwise monotonous 8- to 10-hour workday. My team members' welcome and interactions made me feel like a real team member. When I had the defect flow-out (not setting a clip), the team members reassured me that mistakes happen and not to beat myself up about it. I did inquire of some team members how they viewed the company and management. The consensus of positive feedback was that TMMK's pay and benefits were good and overall it was a good company for which to work. On the negative side, I heard a consistent message that management started valuing output over quality and safety. When I inquired when this value change began, some tenured members said when the Japanese coordinators started leaving.

When TMMK started production in the late 1980s, there were many more TMC Japan coordinators (with strong kaizen minds) on the shopfloor, coaching members and management in operational efficiency and production team member burden reduction through kaizen and problem-solving. As the company rapidly grew (globally), TMMK's Japanese coordinators and support decreased, apparently leaving a noticeable gap at TMMK, perhaps beyond. Some years after that conversation, Akio Toyota also identified this shift in values from safety/quality to output in his (aforementioned) 2010 address to congress.

My Body

For several reasons I found the EMW process physically challenging. The wire harness was a roughly 10-foot bundle of electrical wires near the center of which was a shoebox-sized junction box. It presented draped on a metal rack hook at eye level, like a large snake hanging over a branch. One of the wire harness types weighed nearly 20 pounds with a frequency of about one in every six vehicles, and the remaining were under 15 pounds. I had to flex my shoulders roughly 45 degrees to lift the wire harness and maneuver the dangling wires to avoid stepping on any connectors or terminals that touched the floor on both ends.

To set the junction box in the engine compartment of the vehicle, I had a choice between stepping over the roughly 18-inch-high radiator bar to enter the engine compartment or set it from the outside of the engine room, leaning forward about 20 degrees on the front fender. At Trim 1, the engine was not yet installed, so the compartment space was completely open. I tested both ways and opted to lean forward to avoid the trip hazard of stepping over the radiator bar. Once the junction box was set, there were a dozen electrical wire connectors that had to be set using a push–pull–push motion, which was 36 pinch grips each cycle, but the push–pull–push was an important quality point in assembly especially for parts not designed to give audible or tactile feedback for confirmation of quality. Finally, there were a few work elements inside of the vehicle that required being seated on the metal door frame edge. By the end of my first week, my hands, shoulders, lower back, and backside were extremely sore, and the weekend could not come fast enough.

By the second week, and at the suggestion of a team member, I requested and received a foam rear apron to make sitting on the metal door frame more palatable. For my hands, back, and shoulders, I just powered through, experimenting with various postures that might allow me to recruit larger muscle groups to reduce the physical burden on the smaller ones. I also used any downtime to stretch my limbs and back. I may have conditioned to the physical demands over time, which Toyota refers to as work hardening, but my two-week training time did not permit a test of endurance. Overall, my key development points from being on the production line were greater empathy for the physicality of production work – which otherwise appeared easy – and vulnerability to mental distractions, which lead to defect flow-out (because I could never explain how I missed that clip).

Onboarding Part 3 – Standardized Work "Try on Own"

At the end of my two weeks on the assembly line at TMMK, my next training assignment was to demonstrate standardized work kaizen on the EMW process using the tools and basic schedule from the West Virginia engine facility training. This kaizen activity felt different from my first at the engine plant because there was no group within which to build competition – although I certainly felt that I was competing against the clock. Also, my coaching came from a single person, my assistant manager, who would check in with me every few days to offer support and feedback beginning with "What is the need here?" Still unused to and unprepared for this coaching way, my assistant manager and I bumped heads. I was not given a specific performance target, so I had to research the condition of the process and line to link the kaizen activity to the business need such as safety, quality, productivity, cost, etc.

After researching and capturing the initial condition of the EMW process using the standardized work analysis tools, I chose to focus on reducing muda and the physical burden (e.g., awkward postures and hand forces) that I experienced. I appreciated working on the production line at TMMK, albeit briefly, because that experience profoundly impacted my view and insight into the nuanced and complex interactions between the human body and mind, repetitive work, part quality and condition, and management, all of which change over time, which can increase (or decrease) the risk of injury.

Identifying muda was simple enough – innovating 30 kaizens to reduce muda was not so simple, neither would be conducting the kaizen trials. I got input and feedback from the other team members who performed the process, but there was no consensus on the most burdensome work tasks – and some team members thought the process was fine as it was. The very first kaizens targeted a reduction in the burden of lifting and transporting the boa constrictor-like main wire. One of my first stops was the engine main wire process at the adjacent plant to see if they had a better process, then I could simply yokoten the ideas (or evaluate how it could apply in another area). That was to no avail. Again, I found myself in the middle of a bustling plant left to figure out how to improve a stable process like at the engine plant weeks before. I was praying for a deluge of innovative and creative ideas that could be tested with a zero budget, but I struggled to get going until my assistant manager showed and introduced me to the tool shop and manager. There laid the key that opened my creative and autonomous spirit – tools and maintenance members who enjoyed the challenge of building things like mock-ups. I experimented with makeshift hoists, various techniques for better presentation of parts, transferring and swapping work elements with other processes.

My planned time for kaizen on the line was one week; however, it took two weeks before I was ready to report out to management as some kaizens took longer than expected. For example, I wanted to kaizen the packaging of a part to shave one second off the process cycle time. I had to find and get approval from the quality engineer specialist who "owned" the part, then collaborate with her to run online trials. For tools, racks, and cart changes, I worked with maintenance shop team members (who had limited availability). For one kaizen trial, I had to recruit help from a random person, which was rare to find because most people had full plates. I tested swapping work elements between two different lines (Trim 1 and Trim 2) to determine if the overall ergonomic burden was reduced. By the way, swapping work elements between production lines was never an easy sell to team leaders and group leaders so that kaizen trial required politicking. Other challenges were to properly communicate and plan kaizen trials that did not interrupt normal production, so many were planned and completed during production breaks. I also had to verify quality at the end of any process that was changed – documenting the vehicle numbers for every trial.

At the end of the two weeks I was again exhausted, but I had reduced the EMW process cycle time by 2 seconds and fluctuation by 7 seconds, demonstrated on the standardized work documents. For others, seconds may be a trivial matter, but in TPS every fraction of a second counts especially because of potential to scale the improvement. While I made some improvements to reduce ergonomic burden, the changes were not significant enough to reduce the overall burden score of the process – which rated both the before and after conditions as medium burden.

At the end of the trials, it was time to tell the kaizen story to OMDD and TMMK management in an A3 summary report. I recalled writing my first "A3" while conducting research at the university, so I thought I would be fine with some minor adjustments. The reality is I would learn through a very Socratic yet feeling-very-micro-managed coaching process – again requiring humility and perseverance – that the thinking-behind and language of A3 is very specific in TPS, so truly I had no A3 experience. I realized my natural tendency was to be all-inclusive, perhaps verbose, but Toyota's way was succinct and visual, showing only the key problems, details, and facts mostly with charts and other graphics. Challenged with fitting four weeks of production, kaizen activity, results, learning, and reflection onto an 11 × 17 sheet of paper in a specific language took no less than five major revisions and countless minor revisions. Each revision was based on feedback in question form, such as "How does this statement connect to that one?" "Why did you go in that direction?" "How can I see what you are saying with words?" Eventually, I made my way through far enough to have a usable summary document, but becoming skilled at A3 writing took many project summaries.

Next, it was time to report out on my "try-on-own" kaizen activity to my division general manager, a TMC Japan member and TPS guru. I had already run through my presentation with my assistant manager and manager for several iterations, but I did not know what to expect from my general manager. I had not spent any considerable time with him by that point, but I was told he is very critical and harsh with his feedback. My manager was a bit on the frantic side as if it were his presentation, and I recall him

14 ■ *Toyota's Improvement Thinking from the Inside*

emphasizing "just stick to the facts and flow, everything will be fine." The report-out was planned to begin in a break room for the documentation review then the shopfloor at the EMW process.

For all the preparation and practice runs, my general manager scanned my standardized work documents and A3 for less than 2 minutes. Then, unexpectedly, he asked me if I was able to perform the EMW process. It had been a few weeks since I worked online, but I obliged figuring that my muscle memory would kick in having done the process over 450 times a day for over a week. After getting permission from the team leader and team member, I nervously replaced the normal team member and performed the EMW process for several cycles. After that, I went on to point out my kaizens that were sustained and a few that were not.

Then, unexpectedly, my general manager's attention drew to the cart that held parts for the process. He noticed that a metal hook on the cart had frayed tape around it. The metal hook was designed to attach the cart to the vehicle when the vehicle entered the work pitch to reduce muda of walking for parts. That hook was taped to reduce the likelihood of mutilation (or scratching) of the vehicle's paint under the wheel well, and over time that tape had become noticeably worn. When he pointed out the frayed tape, I acknowledged the risk and said I would take care of it, fastidiously making a note of it on my notepad. Before I finished writing, my general manager had left, then returned with duct tape, dropped down to the concrete floor, and retaped the metal hook himself. My manager and I looked at each other with an "oh no" gaze. In all the scenarios I had planned for in terms of questions and feedback, I could not have predicted that. This was my first of many experiences observing how differently TMC Japan members prioritized shopfloor conditions over reports, presentations, analytics, etc. and embodied the TPS principles, in this case stop and fix problems with urgency to ensure quality. Coupling this embodiment with a stern reproach way of correcting unfit TPS behavior, I had the context to understand the assistant manager's story on the way to the West Virginia engine plant about the TMC Japan executive who walked out of the American supplier meeting.

The Change Point: Double Consciousness and Values

My onboarding experiences rounded out with other standardized work kaizen trainings and an introduction to problem-solving in the vehicle paint shops, all of which were conducted, coached, and emoted in a similar vein. My onboarding experiences in OMDD were full of such unpredictable moments and struggle– to learn, to kaizen, and to fit in – and I was not alone as my cohort shared the sentiment that OMDD's way of challenge was frenzied, deliberately annoying, and inefficiently Socratic onboarding and training – even though they/we consistently achieved improvement results.

In my first six months of learning TPS from the inside, I gained a deeper understanding of some of the TPS tools and methods to improve operational performance, some of which I was already aware of from books, articles, and graduate school classes. What I found profound, however, was the culture and the ways in which OMDD (and other TPS groups) developed team members' capability to improve work, add value for customers, and solve problems compared to my prior experiences at top industry and academic organizations. Their coaching way was consistent with a kung fu sifu whose feedback was periodic and at times felt critical and/or circuitous in order to build both humility and capability in the DNA of its members. Their way was also supportive toward reaching the end goal of performance improvement. Those coaches at one point had gone through the same fire and were battle tested in order to lead others through to the other side with no shortcuts.

I personally struggled to adapt to the culture but came to recognize that the way of OMDD was consistent, genuine, effective, and full of good purpose (not cult-like for the sake of pure capitalism and labor exploitation). And the intense pace and style of coaching was a significant and preserved cultural way based on values and principles that were non-negotiable, intentional, and passed down for decades inside of Toyota to new team members and beyond. The company and system required me to humble myself more than I had ever professionally experienced before in order to fully understand how to successfully navigate its complexity and consistently achieve results. I also realized (from others who seemed to do well in the group) that to be successful on my TPS learning journey, I had to develop a double consciousness – appreciating and adopting Toyota's Japanese ways juxtaposed to my American consciousness – and learn to code switch between the two depending on the situation. Finally, and perhaps most generalizable to the work of improvement, I learned that if someone created the system, and the system encountered problems, then someone should always be able to improve the system so long as that someone had the requisite breadth or depth of knowledge of the system.

The Transformation Model

Having shared the beginning of my TPS journey, let me jump ahead to the end. I continued to develop in the way of operational excellence and high performance – improving my kaizen thinking, problem-solving skills, and ability to lead and develop others along the way inside of Toyota, then eventually outside of the company. I eventually transferred to another division called TSSC, a non-profit division that develops TPS know-how and capability toward the end of organizational transformation for American organizations of various kinds, from manufacturing to healthcare to education. It was there that I gained greater insights into how to apply the thinking in non-Toyota environments. It was there that I realized the thinking can be transferred to any organization, regardless of the product, service, technology, size, location, etc. It was there that I also noticed that traditional thinking to achieve higher performance by investing in high-cost individual contributors (through compensation and bonuses) does not work, and such extrinsic motivation schemes tend to produce a culture of elitism and exclusion and higher turnover, which can negatively impact performance and the bottom line.

Just like fire needs three elements to exist – heat, oxygen, and fuel – I have found three key domains for organizational transformation toward continuous improvement, high reliability, learning organization, etc. The diagram in Figure 1.2 summarizes the domains of my personal transformation that when aligned and scaled leads to organizational transformation into a lean organization, learning organization, high reliability organization, etc., which possesses demonstrable and enduring high performance relative to external competition and for the benefit of customers.

This conceptual model for organizational transformation includes the technical systems, or the tools and capabilities, required to do the work of the organization. This domain is mentioned first because in my experience most organizations want or expect the improvement journey to begin and end in this domain because many technical tools (such as pull system, andon, heijunka, total productive maintenance – explained later) have been the focal point of most of the books and articles written about TPS and the broader lean movement. The problem is that most attempts to adopt only the technical systems have been done so at the surface level and with limited success and an inability to sustain performance improvements over any length of time. I will not assume that all readers are familiar with the

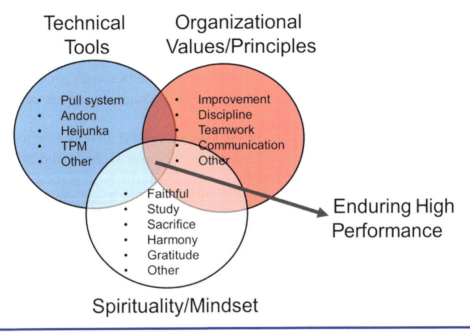

Figure 1.2 **Transformation model**

technical tools and methods, so in the next Chapter I provide an overview of the more popular ones and the basic thinking behind them.

The next domain includes the social systems, specifically the values and principles consistently reinforced by management in the organization. If the transformation model were a physical prepackaged system to plug and play into any organization, this domain would have items in the box that organizational leaders may overlook because their value is not apparent. In an organization there could be as many professed values and principles as there are leaders, and those values typically sound good and noble. What is far more important is how and the extent to which members of the organization experience them. The old adage says that a tree is known by the fruit that it bears. Toyota has many values and principles that are good and noble – two of which (kaizen and respect for people) were succinctly published in an internal document called the "Toyota Way, 2001." A longer list was called out in Jeffrey Liker's book, *The Toyota Way* – values such as taking a long-term view in decision making, making decisions through consensus, growing leaders who understand the work and live the values, etc. As they relate to organizational transformation, specifically, I highlight some key values and principles in the culture of Toyota that emerged during my TPS transformation in the onboarding period and beyond that seemed foundational to high performance, which include improvement, discipline, teamwork, and communication, which are further discussed in the next Chapter.

The third domain to consider in transformation is the spirituality and mindset of the members within, or "how the me becomes a we" in which individuals connect with each other and the higher purpose of the organization.

This is one of the most important yet least discussed aspects of transformation work and perhaps for good reason – religion is typically the proxy for spirituality, and "too much religion" especially in the workplace can be quite divisive and discriminatory. I get it. By spirituality, I am referring to existence that is immaterial but has meaning, purpose, and connection with the material world and how many of us create meaning, purpose, direction, creativity, and innovation in our lives. So, a spiritual mindset refers to a mental inclination toward higher level purpose, thinking, and actions that help us become better versions of ourselves over time so we can better help others. I personally identify as Christian; however, the lens for interpretation is not limited to any specific faith or religion. In fact, there was a diversity of spiritual backgrounds in our TPS group including Buddhist, Hindu, Jewish, Christian, spiritual atheists, non-affiliated spiritualists, and others. In the same way, there were no open discussions on the emotional journey members experience in OMDD; there were also no public conversations about personal spirituality. However, I could sense it was there when we convened and confirmed it in some cases through intimate conversations with members.

Toyota's spiritual roots trace back to Toyota's founder, Sakichi Toyoda, a practicing Buddhist. Among his teachings, he articulated "Five Main Principles" in business conduct, which were posthumously handed down in the company (see https://www.toyota-global.com/company/history_of_toyota/75years/data/conditions/precepts/index.html):

- Always be faithful to your duties, thereby contributing to the company and to the overall good
- Always be studious and creative, striving to stay ahead of the times
- Always be practical and avoid frivolousness
- Always strive to build a homelike atmosphere at work that is warm and friendly
- Always have respect for spiritual matters and remember to be grateful at all times

Another way in which spirituality, which is deeply imbedded in TPS, reaches the surface and can be observed is when you hear members discuss True North thinking. True North is a concept that represents the ideal state of perfection – which in the context of business includes having perfectly defined goals and perfect processes in place to perfectly meet those goals. Just like heaven, there is no earthly arrival at True North, but Toyota members should be striving to getting closer every day.

As I explained in my onboarding experiences in Toyota, developing the right mindset was not an easy road for me (or others) as I felt myself struggling with the technical and temporal challenges presented and disconnected from (actually opposed to) the TPS coaching way, which evokes a wellspring of negative emotions. To overcome and be successful I had to rely upon my spiritual groundings, and by centering spirituality and the ongoing journey to develop myself, specifically my mind, I gained greater understanding, direction, and ideation for leading and conquering some very challenging work. In this way, I regard my learnings and experiences at Toyota as sacred, set apart from traditional ways of thinking about work, practices, and performance. I lived in the struggle – the intersection of these three domains of the transformation model – under some of the best TPS thinkers, and it was there I discovered how quickly our capability for continuous improvement can develop. At the organizational level, the extent to which these three domains align for its members will dictate the magnitude and speed of organizational transformation and enduring high performance. This alignment requires intentionality, so Toyota has committed to developing members who live in the high-performance zone, which has profoundly set the company apart with high performance over time.

Sharing the Good News

My experience inside of the TPS was something unexpected yet powerful, so it is with gratitude, passion, and a sense of community that I share my learnings with others who are interested in systems of improvement and organizational transformation. I do not believe Toyota can be replicated. I do believe the principles and practices of TPS can be adopted in any organization to improve operational performance, with the right thinking and will to do the work, to achieve enduring high performance. I have hope that readers, especially from public-serving institutions who cannot see how high performance in making cars relates to them, will be inspired to use these learnings to help close critical gaps in their operational performance and outcomes. I have seen and experienced some glaring gaps such as poor quality and/or lead times in industry, chronic ER and OR operational problems in hospitals, and neighborhood schools that repeatedly fail to meet state proficiency standards, and it does not have to be this way. The wise and noble Maya Angelou would say, "When we know better, we do better."

It is my goal to encourage people and organizations to do better. Using the transformation model as the framework for transitioning members and the organization itself to achieve enduring high performance, the intent of this book is to:

- Clarify some basic thinking behind Toyota Production System tools, values, and principles in a culture that supports high performance, which, jumping to the end, is obsessed with surfacing and solving problems.
- Deep dive into an example of problem-solving at Toyota.
- Discuss the application of TPS tools and principles outside of Toyota across an array of sectors such as manufacturing, healthcare, and education, including challenges and strategies for aligning the three domains to achieve enduring high performance over time.

Chapter 2

Technical Systems, Values, and a Culture of Improvement

If you Google search Toyota Production System (TPS) or its broader derivate lean production, the number of books, articles, consulting services, etc. is overwhelming. Most descriptions of TPS highlight the various industrial engineering or technical methods used to produce things; however, that is not where the power of TPS lies. Those physical things may be more easily observed from the surface, but the basic thinking, values, and principles and culture behind them are equally important for transformation and performance. As you read this section on the more popular technical systems, keep in mind that while the safety/productivity/quality tools were borne out of the production of things, the basic thinking behind the tools applies to the production of healthcare, education, software, designs, laws, and various kinds of services. I will attempt to provide a technical systems overview in an easily digestible way, especially for the reader outside of the manufacturing world. As you read, keep in mind that because language is such an important aspect of culture, in many instances I use Toyota's vernacular to show honor to the learnings/teachings. Also, their vernacular is often more succinct and simpler, even though it may read clunky and/or poor English – in which case I will include the English translation.

First things first, Toyota developed a framework for learners inside and outside of the company seeking to understand TPS basics and transformation. The framework shown in Figure 2.1 visualizes some of the technical and non-technical concepts resembling a house constructed of elements that work as a system for the purpose of customer satisfaction. At the top of the

DOI: 10.4324/9781003540670-2

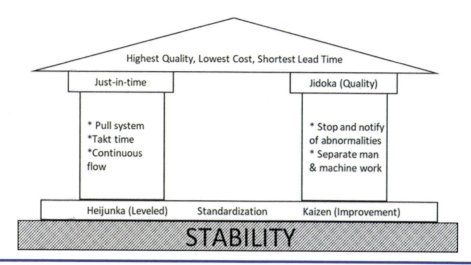

Figure 2.1 TPS house (©TSSC 2000)

TPS house is the ultimate goal of the system, which is to deliver the highest quality, at the lowest cost, and in the shortest lead time. The superlatives of the ultimate goal operate more conceptually than operationally in the TPS journey toward the True North (ideal state of perfection). Practically speaking, customer expectations, market conditions, and regulatory requirements – all of which shift over time and in unpredictable ways – drive the investments, initiatives, and therefore the collective struggle to adjust and adapt as an organization. For many of us it felt like trying to walk along a tightrope whose tension was held on one side by these external forces and our limited way of thinking on the other.

There are two pillars that support the ultimate goal of the production system: *jidoka* (quality) and just-in-time. At the ground level are the concepts of *heijunka* (leveling), standardized work, and *kaizen* (continuous improvement). Finally, the foundation of the house (and the entire system) is the concept of stability. There are many lean manufacturing books that go more deeply into the application of some technical tools of the transformation model, but for our purpose I will give a brief overview of the commonly cited technical tools using a relatable context, that is, a fast-food restaurant. In high school, I worked at a fast-food restaurant not realizing then the trove of operational excellence that would come in handy to explain organizational theory decades later.[2]

The basic operational flow of the restaurant was that a customer placed an order (inside or drive-through), a team member took the order via a computerized order entry system, money was exchanged, and the items in the order populated computer screens that were used in the downstream processes where team members cooked, prepped, and packaged the orders. Minutes later, the customer left the restaurant or drive-through satisfied, usually. Referring to the roof of the TPS house, the ultimate goal of our crew and the system itself was to maintain high customer satisfaction in quality, cost, and order lead time.

Stability and Muda

Starting with the foundation of the TPS house is stability, the concept above which all other TPS concepts and the ultimate goal of customer satisfaction rest. In TPS, stability is operationalized in various ways, but its essence is the extent to which the actual output of the system produces what is planned within the time it is planned and a commonly used measure of stability is operational availability. In the restaurant example, if the target for order lead time was 3 minutes or less per customer, and 9 out of every 10 customers had orders filled within 3 minutes, then the operational availability would be 90%. Pursuit of True North means striving toward 100% operational availability.

Common problems that impact stability include equipment breakdowns, material shortages, poor quality, turnover, absenteeism, etc. These problems create muda, obstruct true efficiency, increase operational costs, reduce profit, and/or get passed on to the customer in higher pricing, longer lead times, and poorer quality. In Toyota, there is an ongoing and concerted effort to reduce muda and improve stability – from implementing policies and nurturing a culture that minimizes absenteeism and turnover, to helping suppliers develop their capability and operational excellence to minimize the risk of material shortages, to maintaining equipment using a total productive maintenance (TPM) approach. TPM is the planning, monitoring, and caring for equipment to ensure good quality, safety, and longevity in the same way that a personal vehicle gets routine maintenance based on the manufacturer's schedule in addition to daily checks (of tires, oil, etc.) by the driver.

Jidoka – Integrating Respect, Quality, and Productivity

Jidoka, a pillar in the TPS house, is a Toyota concept of automation with human sensing – or giving equipment/machines the ability to detect and stop for abnormal conditions such as defects in production. Jidoka thinking dates to Sakichi Toyoda, father of the company, whose many monikers include engineer, inventor, and entrepreneur. In 1867, Sakichi was born into a Japanese farming family and community with modest means. As a young person, he dedicated himself to hard work and the intense study of weaving as a means to improve life for his family and community. The oral tradition of Sakichi is that he would intensely study his mother and other women weaving to develop ways to reduce the physical burden of the process. He invented devices for looms that made weaving more efficient – higher output and less burden on the person – including his fully automated loom in 1924. For the automatic loom, he went on to create a low-cost, low-tech device to detect and stop production in the event of a broken thread (see Figure 2.2), which was a regular and costly occurrence. Sakichi's intense study methods, work ethic, and thinking around building quality (and productivity) into the system was a tradition that continued when the Toyoda family ventured into automobile manufacture.

The pursuit of True North means striving toward 100% quality in products and processes so there is an obsession with error-proofing processes and making abnormal conditions like defects easy to notice so corrective action can be quickly taken. When the system was designed in such a way, team members spent considerably less time monitoring quality and more time responding to abnormalities, thus improving productivity.

Figure 2.2 Replica of Sakichi Toyoda's jidoka device – hundreds of metal pins inserted between each thread on the loom to detect and stop production in the event of a broken thread when weft thread ran out, saving an extraordinary amount of lost time and material and allowed for one person to operate several machines simultaneously. (Photo Source: www.allaboutlean.com)

There were many examples of good jidoka thinking in the fast-food restaurant such as the soda dispenser, which automatically stopped dispensing once the cup was filled to the desired level, freeing the team member to perform other tasks instead of waiting and watching the machine. Another example was the deep fryer, which signaled with an audible sound when the cook time was reached, freeing the team member to perform other tasks (although it was not error proofed to prevent overcooking, as customers may have experienced on occasion).

Just-in-Time

Just-in-time (JIT) is the concept of producing only the right parts, at the right time, in the right quantity to meet the customers' needs – no more, no less on the journey toward True North. Like jidoka, JIT has a Toyota tradition that dates back to Sakichi's son, Kiichiro, who was also an engineer and businessman. Kiichiro founded the Toyota Motor Company (TMC) in 1937 sometime after traveling to North America and Europe to study Henry Ford's automotive production system and admiring the ways in which automobiles and automobile manufacture could advance society. The challenges Kiichiro faced entering a competitive industry led by global players Ford and General Motors cannot be overstated. With investment funds from his father, Sakichi, Kiichiro and his team designed and created their first vehicle, the Toyota model AA, in roughly two years. To be successful in the highly competitive automotive business environment, Kiichiro developed the strategy to offer greater responsiveness and product variety to customers and produce in smaller batch sizes with more frequent changeovers (to keep inventory costs and space requirements low).

Continuous Flow and Takt Time

In pursuit of True North, customer demand should be met with no stagnation (delay) or other forms of muda (waste) in the process, and material and/ or people flow through the system continuously to achieve the shortest possible lead time. This tradition is attributed to Henry Ford's early 1900's automotive production methods and the continuously moving conveyor line from which Toyota leaders learned and modeled production.

In the fast-food restaurant, flow is easy to observe as customers walk in or drive through and a few minutes later they leave with a completed order. Fast food aside, many production systems are much more complex and not designed to complete customer orders first-in first-out, but rather demand is aggregated and filled over a fixed time period. In TPS, the aggregate customer demand rate is referred to as takt time. Takt, a German word for beat or pulse, represents the pace of customer demand and is calculated by dividing the available production time per time period by the customer demand in that time period.

$$\text{Takt time} = \frac{\text{Available production time}}{\text{Customer demand}}$$

As an example, if the restaurant receives roughly 400 customer orders per day and operates for 1,080 minutes per day (6 am to 12 am), then the takt time computes to 2.7 minutes per order. In Toyota production facilities, this metric is used to establish the production line speed (which is typically paced by an automated conveyor system). It is also used as a guide toward True North and the relentless pursuit to run operations at takt time, no faster or slower.

Pull System (like a Supermarket)

Meeting customer requirements in a continuous flow (paced at the takt time) is often too challenging and costly due to many factors such as travel distance, variation in processing times, process reliability, long processing times, etc., so instead customer orders move through the system in batches with inventory (and stagnation) between processes. Taiichi Ohno, who began as a supervisor at Toyota in the 1940s, developed the TPS concept of a pull system to manage production and inventory. The story goes that on a trip to the United States in the 1950s, he visited a supermarket (not then prevalent in Japan) and was inspired by the simplicity of a customer pulling what items were needed, when needed, in the amount needed – then, the pulled inventory was soon replenished on the shelves. This led to the creation of kanban, a key element of a pull system, which is an order card or other signal to communicate what materials to produce or convey to meet customer demand. From a True North perspective, the number of kanban (or inventory) in the system is continuously reducing in order to highlight and reduce muda in the system that the inventory tends to hide.

In the fast-food restaurant, there are demonstrable aspects of the pull system. For example, during peak hours it is typical to carry inventory of the popular sandwiches and French fries. These items are stored in item-specific (dedicated), first-in first-out lanes under a heat lamp located behind the order counter. The team member bagging the order pulls the stocked items (with no wait time) and the signal to replenish the pulled item comes from the order entry system.

Heijunka

Heijunka is another important technical concept in the TPS house. It is a Japanese word that practically translates to leveling the way in which aggregate customer demand is scheduled to be produced, considering both the volume and the variety (or mix) of demand over a fixed time period. The purpose of leveling is to improve overall customer satisfaction, reduce the fluctuation (high and lows) of orders in the supply chain, and minimize total inventory in the system and cost. There are not many obvious examples of this principle in the fast-food restaurant because the system is designed to fulfill customer orders first-in first-out, not aggregated. However, for illustrative purposes let's say heijunka logic was programmed into the restaurant's order entry system. Four different customers place orders at the same time (with four different cashiers) during peak hours when there is inventory of sandwiches (kept under heat lamps). The combined orders included eight hamburger varieties – four large (L), two medium (M), and two small (S) – which were sent electronically to the upstream process, burger-prep. The bagger process can immediately start pulling the items available from the dedicated lanes. To maintain heijunka (leveling) by volume and variety, the burger-prep process replenishes the inventory based on the following order: L, M, L, S then again L, M, L, S. Alternatively, the heijunka logic could have swapped the order of M's and S's for a similar effect. In this way, the overall inventory of burgers in the system and customer wait time (if any) remains low. Also, the impact on the processes supplying burger-prep (e.g., team members who grill the meat) is a smoothed volume of work so it can operate efficiently as well. When the complexity of the system increases from a dozen menu options to hundreds, heijunka thinking results in significant cost savings.

Standardization

Standardization is another important concept in TPS as it helps minimize costs and maintain safety, quality, productivity, and other key performance measures. Standardization is operationalized in many ways at Toyota such as standardized work for takt time processes (discussed in technical detail in the appendix), the ways in which training is conducted, how A3 documents are written, and the list goes on. In the fast-food restaurant there are many examples of standardization such as the customer greeting, uniform clothing, the uniform cash registers, the cleaning standards at closing, and the list goes on.[2]

Many organizations accept standardization as a good idea, just as they accept adding colored lines to the road to ensure safe and efficient driving conditions is a good idea – but many struggle with implementation and/ or sustainability. In Toyota, on the other hand, both management and team members are very clear about the role and importance of standardization, so it feels normative to "stick to the standard," with the exception of a compelling reason to change course. Also, TPS gurus have a unique way of teaching members when the drawn lines are fixed versus when they should be reimagined and redrawn.

Safety and Safe Process Design in Transformation

I joined Toyota with an awareness that some TPS (or lean) practices implemented in industry were linked to a variety of poor safety and health outcomes such as cumulative trauma disorders, job anxiety and depression, fatigue, and heavy workloads. Paul Adler and others published a study discussing the safety concerns at a GM and Toyota joint venture, New United Motor Manufacturing, Inc. or NUMMI, after Cal-OSHA cited the company for not properly addressing ergonomic risks during a 1993 vehicle launch. The authors attributed NUMMI's increased injury rate to poor supplier quality, parts fitting problems, and restrictions placed on job rotation – problems that are rather common especially in manufacturing. Those issues might have been mitigated through management interventions; instead, according to the authors, they were compounded by a dearth of ergonomic expertise and training, management's poor evaluation of ergonomic risk, and slow reaction in addressing reported injuries. If the goal is true transformation, there is a lesson to be learned to stay ahead of safety concerns – that is, it is foundational to consider both the humanity and the physical capability of team members in process design. Sakichi Toyoda deeply studied ways to improve work and reduce burden in weaving and looming, so we must think in the same way.

Ergonomics in Daily Management

At Toyota, there are technical resources to help manage ergonomic concerns and prevent injuries including health and safety professionals with ergonomics training, health clinics, and/or physical therapists at most TPS facilities. Safety and health professionals and production members used an ergonomic evaluation tool developed at TEMA and similar to other industry tools such as ACGIH's Hand Activity Level, Rapid Upper Limb Assessment, or Job Strain Index (ACGIH, 2005; McAtamney & Corlett, 1993; Moore & Garg, 1995) to measure risk exposure. The evaluation tool scored each work element in the process and produced an overall score of red (above the exposure guideline), green (below the exposure guideline), or yellow (between green and red thresholds). Team members were also expected to voice their safety concerns to team leaders (or management), and if they did so on a red process, it was a priority for management to monitor and quickly countermeasure problems.

To help manage the complexity, the basic philosophy for ensuring safe processes included a suite of countermeasure options:

- Coach team members on any key points to maintain more neutral postures
- Coach team members on any knacks that reduce the force required to install parts
- Limit team members' rotation into a red process to only once per shift
- Swap high-risk work elements with those on a less burdensome process
- Temporarily add a team member to a burdensome process to increase rest/recovery until a more permanent countermeasure was established
- Limit which team members perform a process based on body size, also known as job fit
- Kaizen ergonomic concerns with equipment, tooling, layout, and/or part change

Kaizen

Kaizen, the Japanese term for improvement, is the mindset or way of thinking about eliminating muda and improving operational performance. Ohno's

Figure 2.3 Standardization is tied to kaizen

thinking was that every team member every day should look for ways to eliminate muda, and he highlighted seven specific types: people waiting, unnecessary transport of material, unnecessary movement of the body, inefficient processing, extra inventory, defects, and producing more or sooner than the customer needs, which is known as overproduction that hides problems (Ohno, 1988).

Kaizen is the vehicle that drives the organization toward True North, the absolute best we can be at meeting customer needs. The kaizen tradition traces back to the origins of the company and Sakichi Toyoda's continuous improvement of the weaving process. Figure 2.3 visualizes the basic thinking that inextricably links kaizen and standardization – when operational performance improves through kaizen, the changes are standardized until the next kaizen. In this way, performance continuously and noticeably trends in a positive direction. A commonly used expression in Toyota is "there can be no kaizen without standardization!"

Problem-Solving

Problem-solving, while not specifically called out in the TPS house, is very much a part of kaizen thinking, and the two terms are often used interchangeably in Toyota. Problem-solving is used when a process fails to meet its expectations, standards, or target performance level/condition – as visualized in Figure 2.4.

In the TPS, problem-solving is as much about good thinking and methods as it is the results, methods that include making abnormal conditions (or problems) very visible. This is such a distinct cultural aspect of the system

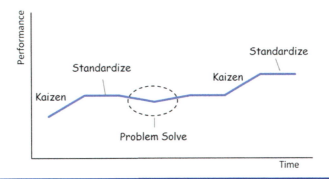

Figure 2.4 **Problem-solving is tied to standards**

considering it is human nature to want to hide problems – which itself is a big problem. Also, there is often a reluctance to deeply study problems and instead settle for "firefighting" or a "band-aid" solution, especially in a busy production environment. Taiichi Ohno, however, emphasized that the most important aspect of problem-solving is to arrive at the root cause, not simply the symptoms of the problem. His practical (yet scientific) approach entailed asking "why" five times to ensure team members get to the true root cause of the problem. From Sakichi to Ohno to now, the basic thinking around problem-solving and kaizen has been constant. Eventually, it evolved into a formalized, company-wide eight-step problem-solving methodology called Toyota Business Practice (TBP), with the customer at the center and root cause analysis still the most difficult hurdle. The TBP method will be discussed in greater detail in a later section.

Another feature of the TPS is that kaizen and problem-solving improvement work on the shopfloor was constant. Whether it was TBP problem-solving training, new hire training, team-based problen solving activities, quality circles, or kaizen leader training, someone somewhere at all levels of the organization was working to improve the system and organization. Root cause problem-solving was one of the most difficult work for me to do, and it took considerable rigor, time, and training to become skilled at it. In addition to the plethora of technical challenges that required innovation and ingenuity to overcome, the TPS culture added socioemotional demands to the improvement process (e.g., do it quickly, cheaply, reliably, humbly, and developing others along the way). This cultural way was and will continue to be one of the most significant contributors to the success of Toyota and its drive toward True North.

In one of the worst of times for Toyota, amid a massive vehicle recall in 2010, TMC CEO Akio Toyoda acknowledged in a US Congressional hearing

32 ■ *Toyota's Improvement Thinking from the Inside*

the tremendous impact of an imbalance between problem-solving development and corporate growth:

> *Today, I would like to focus my comments on three topics – Toyota's basic philosophy regarding quality control, the cause of the recalls, and how we will manage quality control going forward. First, I want to discuss the philosophy of Toyota's quality control. I myself, as well as Toyota, am not perfect. At times, we do find defects. But in such situations, we always stop, strive to understand the problem, and make changes to improve further. In the name of the company, its long-standing tradition and pride, we never run away from our problems or pretend we don't notice them. By making continuous improvements, we aim to continue offering even better products for society. That is the core value we have kept closest to our hearts since the founding days of the company. At Toyota, we believe the key to making quality products is to develop quality people. Each employee thinks about what he or she should do, continuously making improvements, and by doing so, makes even better cars. We have been actively engaged in developing people who share and can execute on this core value. It has been over 50 years since we began selling in this great country, and over 25 years since we started production here. And in the process, we have been able to share this core value with the 200,000 people at Toyota operations, dealers, and suppliers in this country. That is what I am most proud of.*
>
> *Second, I would like to discuss what caused the recall issues we are facing now. Toyota has, for the past few years, been expanding its business rapidly. Quite frankly, I fear the pace at which we have grown may have been too quick. I would like to point out here that Toyota's priority has traditionally been the following: First; Safety, Second; Quality, and Third; Volume. These priorities became confused, and we were not able to stop, think, and make improvements as much as we were able to before, and our basic stance to listen to customers' voices to make better products has weakened somewhat. We pursued growth over the speed at which we were able to develop our people and our organization, and we should sincerely be mindful of that.*
>
> (https://www.cbsnews.com/news/akio-toyoda-congressional-testimo2ny-i-am-deeply-sorry-full-text/)

Culture and Transformational Values

Statistician and management guru Edward Deming said,

> Japan has no natural resources, no coal, no oil, no iron ore, no wood, a little 2222bit of waterpower but they have people and they have good management. And, they have created this world's greatest display of industry out of nothing but people and good management.
>
> (http://www.pqsystems.com/deming)

There is general curiosity and intrigue about Japanese business and management practices. While consulting outside of the Toyota network, I would invariably field questions about Toyota's culture and how it compared to their own organization's culture. When it comes to personal and organizational transformation, culture matters. Merriam-Webster defines culture as the set of shared attitudes, values, goals, and practices that characterizes an organization. Toyota Motor Company in Japan (TMC-Japan) is the epicenter of deep and endeavoring memory of Toyota's values and traditions, especially around True North and kaizen thinking.

As production operations spread abroad, more diversity and cultural heterogeneity were introduced, which required strong leadership support from TMC-Japan in order to maintain the key values. So, when Toyota began producing vehicles in the United States in 1984 at NUMMI, TMC-Japan had sent hundreds of American production members and management to Japan for TPS training and cultural transfusion. They also sent Japanese executives, advisors, and coordinators back to the United States to further support and develop the TPS thinking way and cultural transfusion. I worked at TEMA, a fairly large organization with a distinct culture compared to the typical American organization and specifically in a department that was profoundly different with an interesting blend of Japanese and American values and ways. Some of these differences were immediately noticeable, while others took time to emerge and perhaps only possible through immersion. In both cases, the culture was key to my personal transformation. Starting with the top of the iceberg then descending below the water, the next section summarizes how I experienced the culture at TEMA.

Work Setting

TEMA headquarters had roughly 1700 employees across various departments and divisions. On the campus in northern Kentucky, they occupied two large buildings: the lab, which was home to many of the technical departments such as Production Engineering, Quality, Toyota Supplier Support Center (TSSC), Supplier Commodity Engineering (SCE), and OMDD, and the main building, which housed everyone else such as HR, IT, Finance, Purchasing, etc. The lab was a fairly secured building that required badge access anywhere past the lobby and then again into each department. My badge could access the OMDD office space, which was shared with TSSC and SCE. All three divisions were established to support TPS implementation and kaizen activities. OMDD, modeled after TMC-Japan's Operations Management Consulting Division created by Taiichi Ohno (the father of TPS), supported the advancement of TPS thinking and values within Toyota's north American manufacturing sites. SCE supported TPS implementation and kaizen within Toyota's north American suppliers, and TSSC was the separate non-profit organization that shared a basic level of TPS know-how with American organizations interested in learning. The three TPS groups were each led by senior and highly tenured Japanese men from TMC-Japan with a reputation of being passionate and no-nonsense about TPS and the company itself. The notion of expert was too antithetical to humility to use, but for sure this is where sat some of Toyota's most experienced TPS practitioners, all of which worked directly with Taiichi Ohno (who too had a reputation for being tough yet passionate) or one of his trainees.

The office workspace was consistent with TPS principles – an open layout of rows and columns of desks that allowed anyone to quickly see from the entry door who was present. The walls were plastered with project status documents, reports, schedules, and other OMDD notable information. We also had a large whiteboard with all team members' current and future travel schedule, which was helpful since most of us traveled weekly to the various manufacturing sites. There were two team members per desk (which once I visited Japan, I would learn how relatively opulent such a layout was because in TMC-Japan many members typically share a table and a phone). There were very few (if any) trappings of elitism as executives or other members of management had no special seating or parking spaces. For privacy, we all relied on the availability of a dearth number of conference rooms and a makeshift conference space created from portable office partitions.

Organization Structure and Ways

OMDD was a relatively small division, maintaining about 30 members whose titles primarily included specialist (non-management), assistant manager, manager, assistant general manager, and at the top was the general manager – a position exclusively held by TMC-Japan members. The ratio of direct reports to supervisors was low, mostly 3 or 2 to 1, which was a key feature based on the time- and energy-intensive process to develop members, a primary role for supervisors. OMDD members were from a mix of backgrounds that ranged from recent college graduates to members who had spent many years in manufacturing, and others from various TEMA departments, Toyota suppliers, or affiliates. Between all three TPS groups, I was one of only a handful of women – half of which occupied administrative assistant roles. The work teams in OMDD were organized by manufacturing shop such as stamping, body weld, paint, assembly, logistics, etc., and I was assigned to the paint shop, alongside three other members.

My first week, I noticed a couple of things that left an indelible impression. One, I noticed there were no trash cans at our desks and we had to walk to the garbage and recycle station to discard items. When I was given a building tour, the administrative assistant set the expectation to strictly follow the recycling rules for garbage versus plastics, metals, and compostables – or we could opt to take the trash home, which some members occasionally did. I would eventually visit Japan and experience the care exercised around recycling. For example, on one visit my team was testing out auto parts that were packaged in plastic bags with a paper label stapled to the bag. We were given separate recycle bins for each material, and we were expected to carefully remove the metal staples from each bag then place it in the appropriate receptacle. It took a while for our American team to adjust to such practices.

The second thing I noticed about our office space was how quiet, focused, and guarded were the people who had also maintained a tension that was not easily describable. Occasionally, I would catch banter or laughter, but those moments were brief and rare. The TMC-Japan executives and coordinators (or advisors), while few in numbers, about three in OMDD at any given time, highly influenced the work culture based on their work culture back home. They had the most influence in part because of their status in the formal pecking order, also in part because it was assumed that they were highly capable assets in terms of TPS know-how. Since Toyota's US operational performance lagged significantly behind Japan's across the board

36 ■ *Toyota's Improvement Thinking from the Inside*

(e.g., quality, productivity, safety, cost), we relied on TMC-Japan members for direction, development, and knowledge transfer.

Some American members, including myself, showed deference to Japan members by bowing upon greeting for the first time as it is in the Japanese tradition. We learned to speak a hybrid of Japanese and English because not all Japanese concepts had a perfect English equivalent, and some TMC-Japan members were not exactly confident in their command of English (even when it was very good). When communicating, a few words were always better and pictures or mock-ups were best.

The Japanese members were often the first ones in the office and/or the last ones to leave. I would eventually learn that in Japan, 12- to 14-hour workdays were typical, and when a member leaves the group he/she says goodbye with the expression "osaki ni shitsureshimasu," which literally translates to "sorry to leave before you." At TEMA, however, most members left the office after a nine-hour workday unless there was a serious deadline looming. However, during kaizen activities, the expectation and reality was to spend 12–14 hours each day on the shopfloor; the OMDD team usually arrived and departed together.

Due to travel schedules, it was not often that all OMDD members (especially TMC-Japan members) convened, which limited team-building opportunities; however, some such recurring occasions were the catered new-member welcome lunches, the weekly information-sharing meetings, and monthly one-hour lectures on TPS. For the TPS lectures, a TMC-Japan or senior member of the group presented an example of TPS implementation in the field. Having spent so much time in academia, I felt energized by the lectures as a means to quickly disseminate concepts, experiences, and key learnings not typically covered in the books on lean manufacturing while other members seemed to suffer through them. OMDD members emphasized the basic thinking behind the TPS concept before diving into an example at a detailed, almost minutia, level. Most of the audience took notes during the lecture, including me. This was one of the few spaces to clarify and in some cases debate technical points of the TPS tools, which in the end was typically settled by a TMC-Japan member with a poetic simplicity.

In the weekly division meetings, members shared project status updates and summaries and general administration information. In project reporting, all members were encouraged to respectfully challenge the work of the presenting member with the goal of everyone thinking more deeply about how to improve quality, efficiency, safety, etc. Whether intentional or not, this created a sense of competition between members and subgroups. If a

TMC-Japan coordinator attended the meeting, he would typically offer the final comments/feedback, and when delivering feedback, he would invariably begin with, "Thank you for your hard work," then proceeded to give a simple yet insightful perspective on the TPS matter. I was also warned that when delivering feedback, TMC-Japan members could be direct and harsh.

During my onboarding experiences in OMDD, I thought the work culture, specifically their way of developing people, felt very much like a cult, and my survival in such an environment was quite tenuous. It took me (with a willing heart and eager to learn) six months to a year to grasp the culture and assimilate as I saw the power of their practices in achieving higher levels of performance. I also found that work groups at TEMA, such as OMDD, with strong TMC-Japan leadership and high interaction typically leaned into the power of TPS and had greater cultural homogeneity. Over time, I too would learn how to get results in problem-solving and kaizen activities regardless of how difficult was the challenge. I was also trying to understand the organization's real principles and values, one of the three transformation model domains. There is often dissonance between the values claimed by organization compared to the members' lived experience, so it took time to discover. Over time, some values and principles emerged in my experience that were key for high operational performance, including:

- Improvement thinking: kaizen and problem-solving with urgency, data, challenge, learning, and reflection
- Disciplined way: standardization, perseverance
- Teamwork thinking: respect, humility, autonomy, flexibility, competition
- Communication way: frequent, succinct, visual

Improvement

Kaizen and problem-solving, two sides of the improvement coin, were conducted in a way that really set the TPS culture apart from anything I had ever professionally experienced. The **sense of urgency** with which the activities were conducted was profound – the same urgency with which my general manager took action to fix a quality problem in the middle of my first report-out. Improvement, and work in general, required members to **seek the facts** first, then discuss the issue with data and **not assumptions** or predictions. Another feature of improvement work was to **challenge team members** in order to develop his/her capability and move the organization toward True North. My problem-solving and kaizen assignments were quite challenging as described in my onboarding experiences. In response to challenges, team members were expected to continuously **learn** (with experienced coaching) and demonstrate their capability. Finally, another feature of improvement was **reflection**, the process whereby members were challenged to think deeply about oneself – the thinking, actions, feelings, etc. experienced during the activity – in order to identify opportunities to improve oneself. I describe how these elements play out in a problem-solving example in the next Chapter.

Discipline

The strength of the TPS culture is fully girded by the innumerable ways in which order is maintained through disciplined practices. It started with the organizational structure, which typically included a low ratio of direct reports to supervisors, which enabled the scrutiny and **frequent corrective feedback** required to maintain such order. Also, **standardization** was the way of life on the shopfloor and beyond – from standardized work for hundreds of processes, to standardized locations for storage of parts and materials, to standardized reporting ways, and the list goes on. In the standardized work training, there was a disciplined approach to observing our process, following the protocols for documenting the facts and reporting out. The expectation to keep such order coupled with a challenging work schedule and ambitious targets required **perseverance**, which is a key component of discipline. Team members were expected to and did work (overtime) until the goal was completed, so long days were the norm.

Teamwork

Whether in a production or an office environment, team formation and hierarchy were designed to support the most efficient use of human resources. Team members were trained to be **flexible** in responding to customer needs and internal inefficiencies, from daily overtime of the production line, to team leaders and group leaders who fill in for absenteeism, to me stepping in to run the EMW process at a moment's notice. Between team member flexibility and the top-down, authoritarian development way, team member humility was essential at all levels of the organization. I considered myself **humble** before joining Toyota, but the organization more fully developed my humility as it related to teamwork and team performance. In true team fashion, this humble way was encouraged by the veteran members of the group sharing their stories and experiences from the past and how they triumphed.

If humility is required to strengthen the TPS culture, then **respect** is the yang to its yin – they complement each other. Respect, especially in between-group interactions, played a key part in how members conducted themselves, which depended on the situation and was not always obvious. Respectful behavior was in some cases explicitly taught to new members as in the West Virginian engine facility training when OMDD coaches instructed trainees not to fold our arms during process observations (which sometimes happened naturally after standing for long periods), in order to demonstrate respect for production members who were required to stand for the better part of the shift. Situational respect, however, was usually passed on to new members more subtly as it was the norm for new members to simply follow and observe the senior member. In the engine facility training, for example, I observed how the OMDD coaches demonstrated respect for the facility members by being very gracious, using gentle speech, and communicating frequently with their facility's members and management.

Autonomy (and trust) is an essential aspect of teamwork in TPS, and team members are expected to take ownership of their work and performance outcomes. OMDD supervisors (and coaches) gave feedback, but there was not much hand holding as most members (including management) had full workloads themselves. Juxtaposed to autonomy and promoting accountability, **competition** between members was crafted and used to drive output. For example, in the standardized work training, the team was structured such that each trainee had independent work and goals yet operating toward a common goal (productivity improvement). We posted our progress on the training room walls for everyone to see and twice daily reported our status to the entire group. Whether intentional or not, embedded competition between trainees was palpable, which likely encouraged some members to work more to keep up with the group – at least it did for me.

Communication

Like many organizations, Toyota had a unique communication way from the language itself, which was a hybrid of Japanese and English at TEMA to written communications such as A3 documents. A3s are summary documents written on an 11 x 17 inch paper – the standard for reporting and presenting. John Shook, a former Toyota member, captures the essence of A3 writing in his book *Managing to Learn* (2008). In general, communication

40 ■ *Toyota's Improvement Thinking from the Inside*

tended to be consistent with the theme of muda reduction – that is, **simple and succinct**. It also was frequent (which I initially interpreted as micromanaging). In the standardized work training, coaches (and supervisors, in general) expected **frequent updates** for activity status (and project status) in order to better guide team member actions. This communication way was imparted to new members throughout the training as well as in preparation for any final report-out. In all of my presentations and report-outs, I had at least one coach or supervisor vet the material for key details, flow, and adequate use of **visuals**.

Culture and the Transformation Model

We know that culture matters when it comes to organizational transformation. For example, Liker and Hoseus in *Toyota Culture* (2008) point to the research on cultural differences between Western and Eastern regions of the world and analyze how those differences might impact an organization's adoption of the TPS. If we step down from the organizational level to the individual member, we can more easily see and manage transformation starting with developing the individual member's thinking and kaizen mindset through a variety of purposeful and challenging improvement assignments that clearly connect with the needs of the business or organization (e.g., customer satisfaction, safety, quality, delivery, cost, etc.). At Toyota, coaches play a key role in reinforcing organizational values and principles, keeping members on pace, and carefully managing the tension so as not to create overburden. Such challenges and tension typically and predictably require members to push through negative emotions such as confusion, frustration, overwhelm, etc. to get through to the other side. Whether intentional or not, this experience in many ways mirrors the stages of grief proposed by Kubler-Ross, a psychiatrist who noticed common experiences and coping strategies among patients facing imminent loss of life. She developed a model of these stages, which included denial, anger, bargaining (e.g., mentally negotiating for alternate outcomes), depression, then acceptance (of the reality of loss). The reason her model perfectly fits into the improvement journey is that for transformation of any kind to occur, whether it's a caterpillar transforming into a butterfly or a general leader transforming into continuous improvement leader, something has to die. In TPS, it was the old way of thinking that members had to lose in order to transform – visualized in Figure 2.5. By the way, for most of us, that "old thinking" worked hard

Figure 2.5 **Stages of transformation adapted from Kubler-Ross's stages of grief**

to preserve itself using the strategies of denial, anger, bargaining, perhaps depression, before it (and we) came to accept a new reality.

Which brings us to the significance of spirituality as a powerful force that ties everything together. Spiritual practices (like study, meditation, prayer, sacrifice, etc.) can create fuel out of the negative emotions, create hope that any challenge can be overcome, expand creativity and innovation, and help members get through the stages of grief sooner than later in order to develop a kaizen mind with a greater sense of humility, trust, teamwork, and confidence that is profoundly transformative. It happened for me. It happened for many. It can happen for you and members in your organization. True North thinking is to have every member develop the mindset, but more practically, the extent to which members' kaizen minds are developed across leadership levels within an organization will determine the pace of transformation toward a continuously improving organization.

Chapter 3

Problem-Solving – Oh the Places You'll Go

Many of the technical systems in TPS are designed to reveal problems so action can be quickly taken to resolve issues. In fact, hiding problems would land you in an undesirable place because it contradicts the values and the system and negatively impacts performance. There was a Japanese saying, "having no problems is a very big problem," especially if you are journeying toward the True North. In the same way that my kaizen mind took time and repetition to develop, so did my way of solving problems. Whether solo or on a team, on the shopfloor or in an office setting, problem-solving is one of the most useful skills to develop in organizational transformation. This Chapter deeply dives into a problem-solving example in manufacturing at Toyota to demonstrate the expected way (e.g., speed and rigor) of such activities that are designed to develop members, foster teamwork, and improve operations.

Before we jump into the problem-solving example, there are two management principles and other contextualizing backgrounds that should be reiterated and clarified, starting with the philosophy of standardization at the process level. Standardization helps ensure that improvements previously implemented or newly implemented will be sustained and therefore should be implemented as a necessary pre-condition to problem-solving. The next management principle is measurement. If your organization or group does not track any key performance indicators (KPIs), then this would be a good first step toward transformation. At Toyota, all the shops, departments, and divisions have KPIs that are measured and tracked over time such as safety,

42

DOI: 10.4324/9781003540670-3

quality, productivity, on-time delivery, cost, etc. Those KPIs typically have target performance levels that are determined annually during a (*hoshin*) management planning process and based on some thinking around past performance, benchmarks, business needs, regulatory requirements, etc. Some KPIs were deliberately set to challenging (or stretch) levels in the spirit of the True North and team member capability development, and some targets were practically set to get closer to TMC-Japan operational performance levels. By the way, in Toyota, no one gets fired for not meeting operational performance targets. (They may, however, be put on a performance development plan.) The main point is both standardization and KPI tracking help create system stability and visualize performance gaps for any problem-solving effort.

Paint Shop Overview

Assigned to OMDD's paint group, my primary role was to coordinate, support, and develop leaders in cost-reducing quality and productivity improvements across Toyota's North American paint shops. Vehicle paint is an important aesthetic and quality feature for car buyers as it not only looks good but also vitally protects the metal shell body underneath. The paint shop itself is a fascinating display of engineering, chemistry, and artistry. You can Google search automotive paint processes and watch videos that capture the various processes. Most of the value-added work is performed by automation – dozens of robotic arms, hundreds of spray nozzles, hundreds of thousands of gallons of cleaning and paint solutions in tanks and drums, and miles of conveyor chains that transport the vehicle shell body throughout the paint system. The conveyor process starts with a deluge of water to remove debris and oil from the vehicle body. It then travels through the conveyor system, gets dipped into a series of chemical tanks that treat the metal with anti-corrosion and paint-adhering coats that get cured in heated tunnels called ovens. The metal joints and other openings get watertight seals. Then, the vehicle travels by a conveyor through a series of paint booths and ovens for a primer, top coat and clear coat of paint – which finally brings the vehicle shell body to life. Due to automation, most of the paint shop feels like a lonely place (unlike assembly shops, which are full of team members). However, there are a few processes where team members manually spray paint and apply sealants and perform 100% inspection and

44 ■ *Toyota's Improvement Thinking from the Inside*

repair work. The most notorious visual defects that paint shops aim to eliminate include:

- Debris under the paint such as metal chips, paint chips, dried sealer, and lint/fibers
- Disruptions in paint evenness such as craters, drips, and spits
- Distortions in paint color such as mottle and cloudiness
- Mechanical force-related problems such as scratches and dents

To maintain quality and productivity, Toyota has many standards for team members, processes, equipment, and maintenance. For example, every paint shop requires lint-free coveralls, shoe protectors, and hair nets to enter the paint shop. Upon entry, members proceed through a high-powered air booth with sticky floor matting to remove and capture loose debris on their person. Another universal policy is no touch of the vehicle unless necessary and with approved gloves because oils from the hand can contaminate the paint application. Some shops have unique practices such as restrictions on personal hygiene products that are known to react to wet paint such as silicone products. Other shops require a panel test for anyone interacting with vehicles, in which the team members touch a metal panel and shake their coverall sleeves over it. If the panel after being sprayed with paint shows cratering, the team members follow a cleaning protocol. Additionally, there are many standards for replacing filters, cleaning equipment, and performing routine maintenance.

Problem-Solving in Jishuken

Jishuken, a Japanese term for self-learning, was a (typically) one-week-long team-based problem-solving activity where a dozen or so members converged in a specific location to find and fix issues. You may have heard of the term "kaizen blitz," same vein. There were roughly 6–12 jishukens per year across the various North American paint shops, scheduled during TEMA's annual planning period. Paintshop jishuken participants, typically 9–12 people for each activity, were primarily members from the host shop with a couple from other facilities across North America. Participants were generally chosen based on their developmental needs, availability, or subject matter expertise. OMDD and the host site were responsible for jishuken preparation (typically a few three weeks prior) and the activity itself. OMDD's strength and role was to participate and coach leadership at the host site in root cause problem-solving and telling the problem-solving story with documents and artifacts. At the conclusion of the activity there was a final report-out where the host leader and participants would present their work, learning, and results to top management and TMC-Japan members. Finally, top management and TMC-Japan members would give their developmental feedback and remarks of gratitude. Back at TEMA, OMDD members would summarize the activity, results, and key learnings on a second A3 document, as well as follow up with the host site management on any homework items left. This was the cycle of learning for problem-solving in an area that I initially knew little to nothing about, but that did not matter because the problem-solving thinking way is intended to be transferable. Over time, I learned the paint system, quality gate thinking, and how to get and teach other others to get improvement results in a challenging and complex system.

As was the case with kaizen activities, my former knowledge or experience did not initially prepare me for the speed, depth, and low-cost innovation way with which problem-solving activities were conducted. My first jishuken preparation activity felt frenzy-paced (almost chaotic) over long days, and in typical OMDD's training way, no detailed plan was provided ahead of the activity – although I am sure our coach actually had a plan and/or at least a destination in mind. It was a learn-by-doing, if-you-know-it-show-it, initiation into problem-solving.

The first step in preparing for the jishuken activity was meeting with the hosting paint shop manager to discuss his thinking way and *nemawashi* (Japanese for getting agreement and on the same page) to arrive at a theme, or focus, and plan for the activity. My first jishuken was an important cultural learning moment for me, specifically, observing how OMDD which was an "outsider" group, develops TPS thinking in others and with no formal authority. I figured that it could not be in the form of TPS lectures or a ninjutsu way of development, and it was not. I would describe most interactions with leadership at the host site as having a respectful tension. Although the company's top management agreed to conduct these activities, the members we directly worked with were not always sold on the idea, timing, or OMDD's high standards for improvement work. In many cases, it was stressful enough for the shop managers to meet meet daily production goals in the presence of manpower and material shortages, safety issues, defects, equipment downtime, etc. Preparing for a jishuken in some cases added to the burden and created tension. I would learn there was no precise

46 ■ *Toyota's Improvement Thinking from the Inside*

roadmap for navigating the resistance we met as outsiders, but one way to keep the work progressing included escalating the concern through higher level OMDD management who would meet with the higher level shop management and allow the message to trickle down to the shop leader. This was rare but did happen. The other and most likely pathway to progression was for OMDD to do the lion's share of the preparation work with some support from the shop and to communicate frequently (at least daily) with the jishuken leader on progress. Ideally, these roles would be reversed.

The rest of jishuken preparation consisted of observing operations, collecting relevant data, prioritizing the problems/issues, and selecting the specific jishuken focus. Problem-solving to improve quality in a paint shop had unique challenges because most paint defects required being within inches of the inspection surface and with sufficient lighting to notice them. There was also the difficulty in observing the entire system. Much of the value-added work was performed by automation in restricted access areas such as the ovens and robot zones. Light curtains enclose these spaces, so if someone goes too far, the moving line (or conveyor) stops, in the same way a garage door sensor trips. I tripped my fair share of light curtains during problem-solving activities. It was not a good feeling to mistakenly disrupt production, so I learned quickly how to safely navigate in sometimes tight, dark, and potentially hazardous spaces. Based on these challenges paint shop problem-solving activities often played out much like the steps in crime scene investigations with systematic data collection and deductive reasoning to make sense of the facts to find the non-conformance culprits. So, let's dive into a problem-solving example from a paint shop jishuken that is fictitious but tracks in a real way and follows Toyota's eight-step problem-solving approach.

Step 1: Clarify the Problem

To prepare for the jishuken, we visited the paint shop, which is a very big place with many moving parts. We observed vehicles flowing for the most part, but we also saw muda (waste) such as occasions when the moving line stopped, repairs performed on the vehicle while it moved on the conveyor line (in-line), and repairs performed on vehicles that were taken off of the line (off-line). We worked with one or more leaders in the shop to clarify the ultimate goal of our jishuken work. A universal goal of all jishukens is for participants to learn. But the ultimate goal should have a customer focus and more specific than "highest quality, shortest lead time, lowest cost." Through

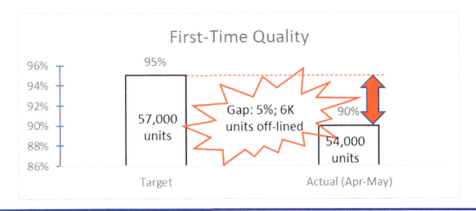

Figure 3.1 Visualizing the gap using a key performance indicator

deep study of the shop, we would arrive at this ultimate goal: support paint quality improvement to reduce repair work manpower needs.

So how much muda was it? To answer this question, we examined the KPIs that the shop's management already tracked, and it turned out the shop tracked several quality KPIs. We met with their management who prioritized "first-time quality" percentage, which is calculated by dividing the number of vehicles that did not go off-line for repair by the total number of vehicles in a shift. Their target was 95% (yes, less than the ideal of 100%). The shop used Microsoft Excel to track information for each vehicle that went off-line including vehicle body number, (suspected) type of defect, location on the vehicle body, vehicle paint color, date and shift, etc. Based on the data, 6,000 vehicles went off-line from April through June of that year. According to production control data, 60,000 vehicles had run over the same three-month period. Therefore, the paint shop's actual condition for first-time quality was 90% (= 54,000/60,000). Comparing management's target of 95% to the actual condition, we arrived at a 5% gap, which is visualized on the graph displayed in Figure 3.1.

Step 2: Break Down the Problem

The next step was to break the big problem down into smaller and more manageable (groups of) problems. We did this by examining and subgrouping the data to determine if there were any noticeable differences between subgroups such as:

- Vehicle model (model A vs. model B)
- Paint color (red vs. white vs. black, etc.)

- Type of defect
- Location of defect
- Work shift
- Any combination of factors

I should mention that statistical terms like p-value, power, and significance were typically not in the conversation, and hopefully it will become clear why that is so. This step was as much about right sizing the scope of the work ahead as it was investigating the underlying phenomena resulting in defects. So, after examining the data in various ways, only one noticeable difference emerged, which was the defect type. Although there was no noticeable difference between the two vehicle types (model A vs. model B), we visualized model subgrouping because of processing differences between the two. We ordered the defects on a Pareto chart (see Figure 3.2), which clearly showed that defect A, craters in the paint, had the highest prevalence (and impact). It was therefore chosen as the primary defect (or culprit) to pursue, contributing an estimated 2.8% (= 1,675/60,000) loss in first-time quality. We confirmed that the shape of the Pareto chart made sense based on our own observations and the production team members' experience.

Once it was decided to focus on crater defects, we further reduced the problem scope to a specific location on the vehicle body. Based on the same data set, the hood and roof had more defects than any other body panel (and the greatest surface areas); see Figure 3.3.

Between the two, the hood was easier to access from anywhere on the moving line (the roof required a raised platform) and could be removed from the vehicle body should a special off-line study be required. Therefore,

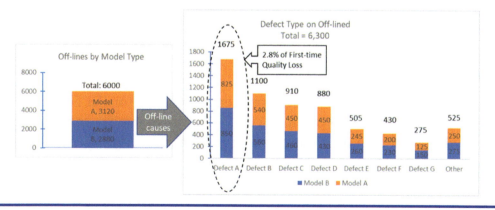

Figure 3.2 Breakdown of the off-lined vehicles by model and defect type

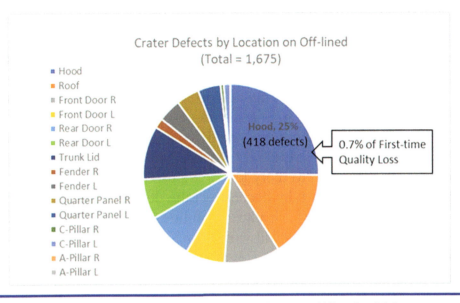

Figure 3.3 Breakdown of crater defects by location on off-lined vehicles

we further reduced the problem scope to crater defects on the hood, expecting a 0.7% (= 25% of 2.8%) impact on the quality gap.

Arriving at this problem focus took roughly one week. Time mattered because we only had three weeks to prepare for the actual jishuken. Most of our time was spent on the shopfloor, observing all the inputs that drove us to the focus area. It was not sufficient to trust that the data collected was accurate; it had to be verified through observation, which meant going to the shopfloor to see where, by whom, and how data were collected. In this case, a team member who worked in an off-line repair process (not paced by the conveyor) inspected the vehicle, performed the defect repair, and electronically logged the repair data, which included his/her experiential judgment of the type of defect. I was skeptical of the categorization of defect type but trusted the completeness of the other data. This was contrasted with another jishuken preparation activity where I found a significant difference in the computer-entered data and what I observed. In that situation, the team member had less time to enter defect data and de-prioritized data entry over keeping the line moving.

To better grasp the facts around why and by whom defects were sent off-line for repair, we went upstream to the final inspection line. We observed all the team members performing their standardized work for each inspection and repair process, paying special attention to the processes that inspected the hood. We noticed that the decision to off-line a defect/vehicle was subjective, based on the experience and judgment of the team members (opposed to a measurement). We also verified with the off-line repair team member that most of the defects sent off-line were legitimate based on the established quality criteria.

To understand the nature of crater defects on the hood, we investigated the physical characteristics (e.g., size, texture, shape, color, etc.) of actual off-lined defects. This required crime scene investigation-like skills and deductive reasoning because the creation of defects could have occurred hours to days prior, depending on inventory levels. We used microscopes, sandpaper, and dissection tools to carefully deconstruct the defect and determine in which layer of paint it rested. Ideally, the off-line repair team member would do this work, but he often had full work doing repairs and limited time for analytics.

Figure 3.4 visualizes the paint applications on top of the metal body in a defect-free (OK) condition compared to an abnormal (no-good) condition in which a foreign substance or material was introduced in the process. To determine in what layer of paint crater defects on the hood occurred, we gently sanded over the defects to remove each paint layer until the defect could no longer be seen with the microscope. The defect in the example in Figure 3.4 was observable under the microscope until we sanded down to the electrodeposition coat; therefore, we deduced it was created after that process. Personally, this cross-sectional analysis skill and confidence took time for me to develop with the help of experienced paint team members.

We performed the defect cross-sectional analysis for a sample of ten hoods that had a total of 11 crater defects (see Figure 3.5). The data showed that the majority (73%) of crater defects were introduced in the primer process, while 27% were created in the top coat process. Thus, we further

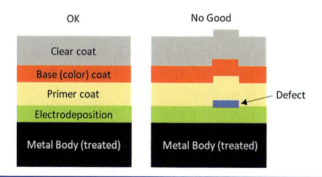

Figure 3.4 Normal versus abnormal paint layering

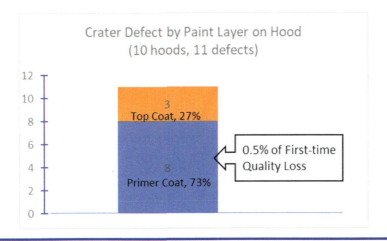

Figure 3.5 Breakdown of defect by paint layer

narrowed our focus to the primer coat area, which had an estimated 0.5% contribution to the quality gap (or 73% of the 0.7 first-time quality loss).

We mapped the location of defects A's to see if a noticeable pattern emerged; however, they appeared to be randomly spread about the hood as in Figure 3.6. Other defect characteristics such as color, size, and shape did not reveal anyt substantial differences.

The next step was to observe in the prioritized area, primer coating process, studying the physical layout, the processes, and the standardized work performed by team members. We met with the team leader of the area to explain our study, make everyone aware of our effort, and get their support where possible. Figure 3.7 shows the high-level flow for primer application, which included both manual processes (with team members) and automated

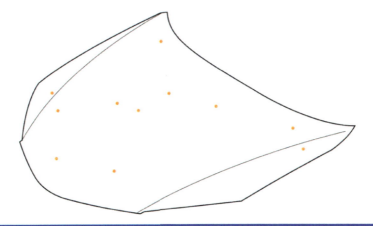

Figure 3.6 Scatter plot of crater defects on (*n* = 10) off-lined hoods

Figure 3.7 Primer application processes and baseline inspection points

(robotic arm spraying) processes. The inspector icons represent inspection locations where one or two jishuken team members captured data near the entrance and exit of primer application. To grasp the current condition of primer process quality, we created a sub-KPI, hood crater defects per unit, and took baseline measures of detectable defects on the hood of vehicles at the end of the primer paint application. . For the baseline data we also created a quality gate by cleaning the hoods of each vehicle to ensure good quality entered the primer system in the baseline study of 20 vehicles; then we inspected the same hoods exiting the system.

The baseline defect rate for the hood was 0.8 defects per unit exiting primer application. We also measured defects entering the primer application and observed 0.2 defects per unit, suggesting that somewhere in the primer process 0.6 defects per unit were being created. The 0.8 defects per unit rate was orders of magnitude higher than the estimated defect rate for off-lined hoods of 0.007 (= 418 hoods/60,000 total vehicles) at the final inspection area. This difference was mostly explained by the fact that some primer defects were repaired online and some primer defects were sufficiently covered/corrected by downstream paint applications (e.g., topcoat, clear coat).

During the weeklong jishuken activity we had more team members available to continue to break down the problem.

We investigated in which primer processes defects were created by performing a series of trial studies with management's involvement. We "shut off" each one of the seven automated or manual processes in the system, one by one, to understand its effect on the defect rate. In scientific method speak, our null and competing hypotheses were:

H_0: no change in defect rate by "shutting off" the process
H_1: reduction in defect rate by "shutting off" the process

By the way, an increase in defect rate was not so concerning; in fact, we might have expected an increase in defect rate from simply introducing more people and opportunities for quality problems into the system. As one paint shop manager once quipped, "I know how to improve our quality, we can stop doing jishukens!" To be empathetic, jishuken activities did bring in more visitors, thus introducing change and a greater chance for contaminants. Particularly vulnerable were shops that did not have robust quality control procedures. Another burden introduced during problem-solving and kaizen activities was change point management. When a standard process was interrupted, such as "turning off" processes for kaizen and problem-solving trials, the shop management was responsible for ensuring changes were documented and tracked the changes, and ensuring good quality by extra scutiny and confirmation checks of the vehicles involved.

The results of the seven trials suggested that Process 1 and Process 5 were the areas of concern. When the two processes were "turned off," the defect per unit on the hood dropped significantly – see Figure A9 in the appendix for the data. Thus, those two processes had become the prioritized areas with the next step to determine what in the process introduced defects.

Step 3: Target Setting

The initial condition for our sub-KPI, crater defects on the hood created in primer application, was 0.6 defects per unit (which was 75% of the total defects leaving primer application). Our target was 100% quality output from the process; therefore, we aimed to reduce primer process defect rate to zero, especially focusing on the two processing areas. If that target could be achieved, we estimated an overall improvement to our first-time quality percentage of 0.38 (= 0.75 × 0.5% first-time quality loss) as shown in Figure 3.8. This targeted improvement would close 7.6% of the quality gap from one jishuken team (among several) during one jishuken activity.

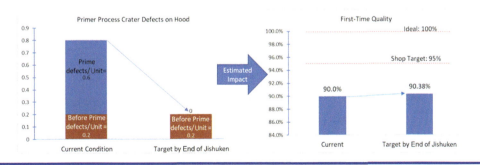

Figure 3.8 Sub-KPI and estimated main KPI targets for the jishuken activity

Step 4: Root Cause Analysis

The next step in problem-solving is finding the root cause or underlying phenomena down to the root. There was (and is) often subjectivity in what is an acceptable depth of causal analysis (e.g., five whys); however, ideally the direct cause of the problem is found and can be demonstrated by turning the cause and problem "on and off." Of course, turning a problem on is not always feasible depending on the situation and cost (in dollars, time, safety, etc.) of the analysis. In our example, the heavy lifting was narrowing down the large vague problem to specific issue and location but not a level of problem specificity that would allow for a root cause analysis.

In an environment where it is difficult to see the problem(s), it was helpful to think in terms of the fishbone diagram (see Figure 3.9), a simple and effective tool created by Kaoru Ishikawa, when brainstorming potential causes of a problem. We began our systematic investigation of the various components of the system (e.g., persons, methods, materials, machines/equipment, and environment) to evaluate what factors significantly impact the measured outcome.

In primer Processes 1 and 5, we investigated many factors such as team members' gloves, equipment cleanliness, air pollutants, etc., and the one examination that revealed a no-good condition was paint contaminants from team members. Two of the four team members in Process 1 failed the panel test for contaminants. In panel testing, team members touched the panel with bare hands and shook their coverall sleeves over a metal panel that was then painted to check if there was a reaction. It was a surprise to the team members that they tested positive for paint contaminants. To confirm, we evaluated the defect rate without the team members in question and observed a slight reduction. This was our prioritized problem at its point of occurence and entry point into five-why analyses. Figure 3.10 shows the five-why analysis for the team member contaminant problem.

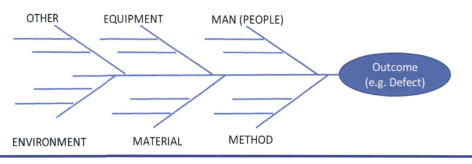

Figure 3.9 **Fishbone diagram example**

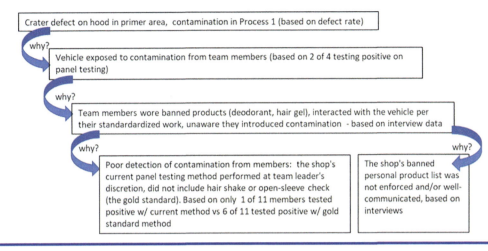

Figure 3.10 Root cause analysis for defects in Process 1

In a similar way, we investigated many factors to determine the cause of defects in Process 5, a fully automated robot zone. A maintenance member discovered a leak in a robot arm spray valve that allowed solvent, which is a paint contaminant, to drip in very small amounts from the nozzle, thus creating defects. To verify, we shut the solvent line off completely and immediately saw a reduction in defect rate. This was our next prioritized problem at its point of occurence and entry point into five-why analyses for defect flow-out in Process 5. Figure 3.11 shows the breakdown for defects flowing out of the process.

Root cause analysis using five-why's is a skill developed with experience. A well-written root cause analysis was evidence-based or data driven as well

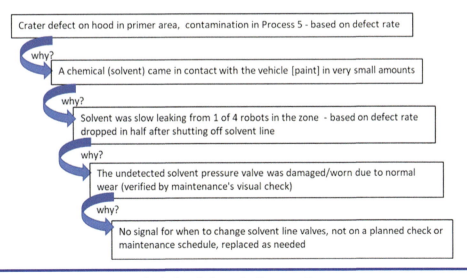

Figure 3.11 Root cause analysis for defects in Process 5

56 ■ *Toyota's Improvement Thinking from the Inside*

as it made logical sense. A check to test the logic is to read each cause in reverse order using a "because" or "therefore" to connect each causal link. For example, to check the root cause analysis in Figure 3.11, we read the following:

> **Because** robot solvent pressure valves were replaced case by case, production ran with an (undetected) damaged valve. **Because** the valve was worn, it slowly leaked solvent from the robot nozzle. **Because** solvent leaked from the robot nozzle, it (sometimes) contacted the vehicle's paint and created defects.

The logic held up reading the causal links in reverse order. It is important to note that in testing logic by reverse order, we test reasonableness that the causal event *could have* happened, if was not directly observed.

At Toyota, I peer-reviewed many TBPs (or 8-step A3's) and noticed how easy it isto go down the wrong rabbit hole in getting to root cause. Take, for example, a root cause identified in Process 1's analysis (Figure 3.10): "the shop's banned personal product list was not enforced and/or well communicated," according to some team members. We could have continued to ask why to delve into social, emotional, and/or cultural issues, but we did not for a couple of reasons. First, we would have needed supporting data on socio-emotional constructs, typically measured using survey instruments that we did not have available within our limits of time. Secondly, because quality is so ingrained into the TPS and culture, our shared experience was that team members would make better choices if they could simply see the link between their choices and quality outcomes.

Steps 5 and 6: Develop and Implement Countermeasures

The next step is to quickly develop and implement countermeasures for the root causes (or upper-level causes). In general, it is good practice to generate as many possible countermeasures as time permits and evaluate the merits of each based on cost, effectiveness, timing, or other considerations. Figure 3.12 summarizes the list of countermeasures developed by the jishuken team.

We discussed (using actual data and facts where possible) the countermeasure ideas with the paint shop leaders, team members, and maintenance to arrive at a reasonable judgment for each and its overall rating. Evaluations were typically summarized using visual and simple symbols: circle, triangle,

Root Cause	Countermeasure (C/M)	Cost	Effective	Timing	Overall
Poor detection of contamination from members	1. Adopt the gold standard method for panel testing	○	△	○	○
The shop's banned personal product list was not enforced and/or well-communicated	2. Review banned product list and corrective actions with 100% of team members - get signatures for acceptance and confirmation	○	△	○	○
No signal or schedule to change solvent line valves	3. Temporary: shut down solvent lines	○	○	○	○
	4. Check for & replace worn valves in entire system	○	○	△	○
	5. Place solvent line valves on a TPM plan	○	○	X	△

Figure 3.12 Countermeasure evaluation matrix (circle = acceptable; X = no good; triangle = moderate)

and "X." The circle denoted an acceptable condition (referred to as "OK"), the "X" denoted an unacceptable condition (referred to as "no good" or "NG"), while the triangle denoted a condition somewhere between the other two.

The next step was to create a plan or schedule for the countermeasure implementation. Figure 3.13 summarizes the jishuken countermeasure schedule and responsible team members. This schedule was also used by OMDD and others as a management tool to follow up with responsible persons once the jishuken week concluded.

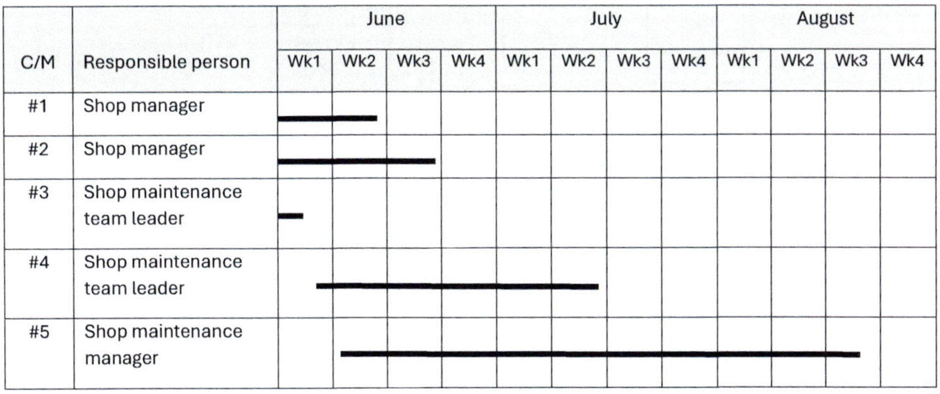

C/M	Responsible person	June				July				August			
		Wk1	Wk2	Wk3	Wk4	Wk1	Wk2	Wk3	Wk4	Wk1	Wk2	Wk3	Wk4
#1	Shop manager												
#2	Shop manager												
#3	Shop maintenance team leader												
#4	Shop maintenance team leader												
#5	Shop maintenance manager												

Figure 3.13 The countermeasure implementation schedule

Steps 7 and 8: Monitor the Results/Processes and Standardize

The next problem-solving step was to monitor the results and the processes that changed or were impacted by changes. Our main KPI, first-time quality, was tracked daily during the jishuken week, so it was not difficult to show the trend over time and annotated with the known system changes. The results for first-time quality in are summarized in Figure 3.14.

There was an improvement from a baseline of 90.0% to 90.9% after some countermeasure implementation for the one-week jishuken. It was not uncommon to achieve performance above the jishuken target so long as the actual root cause had effective countermeasures primarily because countermeasures tend to impact beyond our narrowly scoped focus (e.g., only the vehicle's hood). It was the shop management's responsibility to continue to complete the follow-up items including standardizing the changes, as well as monitor the impacted processes and results. While the improvement closed 9% of the total quality gap, significant in a system constantly endeavoring to close all performance gaps in pursuit of True North, it was not quite enough to reduce off-line repair manpower. There was more learning and improvement work to do.

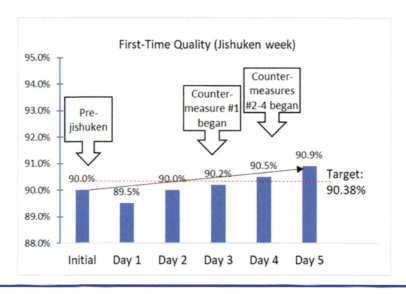

Figure 3.14   Monitoring the results

Storytelling and Report-Out

Jishukens ritualistically concluded with a report-out (or presentation) to a small crowd of upper management and other members. OMDD members helped support the flow of the report-out by working with jishuken team members on how to visualize the data and tell the problem-solving story using flip charts, documents, and show-and-tell examples in or near the activity area. Because the problem-solving activity was focused so much on learning, it was customary for participants to share their key reflections and/or learnings from the activity in addition to the results. OMDD's standard for reflections was high – requiring a deep examination of oneself to identify any known gaps in attitude, knowledge, performance, etc. that might be improved upon in future activities. This explicit expression was one of the ways in which humility and improvement culture was reinforced. The invited members from other Toyota paint shops were given the opportunity to discuss how to yokoten (spread) the learnings to their home shop.

The report-out concluded with upper management giving feedback and thanking everyone for their hard work.

After the jishuken week, OMDD members created an A3 summary of the activity to share our learning with our members and management. Figure 3.15 is an example A3 summary for the fictitious jishuken activity whose story followed the flow of the problem-solving work, intentionally succinct and limited to the key points that fit on the sheet. Charts and other graphical data described previously were read from left to right and top to bottom.

Conclusion

This problem-solving deep dive was intended to demonstrate the rigor, discipline, and creativity that was part of the learning journey that enables enduring high performance for the organization. I focused more on the technical skills of problem-solving and less on the social-spiritual aspects, but these domains are very much part of the magic of TPS. John Shook, a former Toyota member and author of *Managing to Learn*, deep dives into the social-emotional navigation and way finding for members' coaching and being coached in problem-solving development. Similarly, Tracey Richardson through a first-person account in *The Toyota Engagement Equation* dives into the cultural nuance with which problem-solving is learned and

60 ■ *Toyota's Improvement Thinking from the Inside*

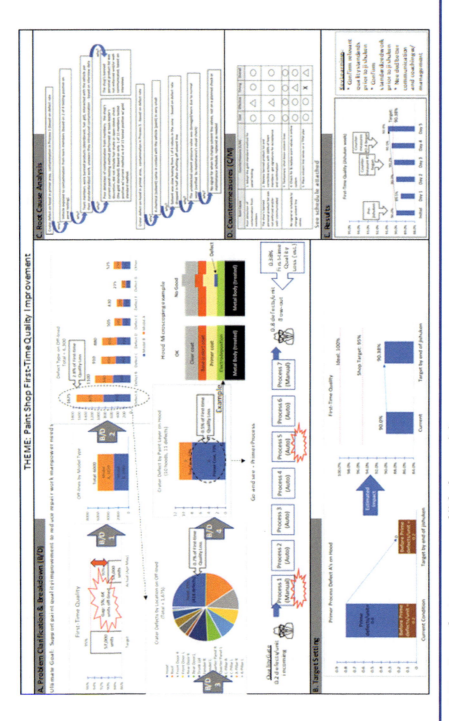

Figure 3.15 Example A3 summary of jishuken activity

conducted at Toyota. Just as in kaizen activities and training, some TPS expectations to think about around problem solving are summarized below.

- Some problems require going places that are uncomfortable so never think, "that's not my job"
- 8-step problem-solving should feel unfamiliar and challenging, requiring members to tear down existing mental boundaries and create new pathways for innovation and creativity. As the saying goes, if you do what you have always done, you will get what you have always gotten
- Moving with urgency and quick action in investigations and countermeasures solves today's problem - tomorrow's problem may be different
- It is all about data - with direct observation and deep understanding preferred over statistical power
- Ideally, all members should develop problem-solving capability, not exclusively those in management or with specialized technical training (e.g., I had no training in paint systems before participating in paint jishukens)
- Systemic problems are solved in a team, with manymembers contributing and working together to innovate, exchange ideas, and nemawashi with management support
- Management is ultimately responsible for the output of the problem-solving activity, which includes both results and team member learning
- Kaizen and problem-solving confidence and capability is a natural output of the aforementioned and lead to high performance

Chapter 4

Continuous Improvement (CI) Implementation in Other Organizations (Manufacturing)

Many individuals and organizations are interested in learning from Toyota ways to continuously improve quality and productivity, reduce wasteful costs, and perhaps continuously adapt as an organization in a competitive environment. As a consultant in Toyota Production System Support Center (TSSC), our mission was to share TPS know-how with a variety of organizations in manufacturing, food processing, healthcare, education, construction, non-profits, and the list goes on. The goal with each organization was neither cultural change nor the implementation of a particular set of TPS technical tools. Rather, we held the hope that we could change the organization's way of thinking toward a kaizen and problem-solving mindset, one member or group at a time as we coached them through their journey – and as individual members transformed there would be a tipping point beyond which the organization's culture would transform with measured and improved performance outcomes. As for the technical tools of TPS, they served as a good entry point for us to engage knowing that Toyota's unique transformation way would be unsettling in the prevailing Western organizational thought and culture.

Using the transformation model as a lens, the purpose of this section is to share insights into the world of continuous improvement transformation

62

DOI: 10.4324/9781003540670-4

Creation of a Continuous Improvement Model

outside of Toyota to glean from others' successes and common pitfalls, in hopes of making your improvement journey more likely to succeed. The first case study takes place in a manufacturing environment, the birthplace of widespread continuous improvement thinking.

Creation of a Continuous Improvement Model

The organization was a high-voltage electrical equipment manufacturer located in the United States, fictitiously named Guiding Electric (GE). GE manufactured a vast array of high-voltage electrical system products, such as pad-mounted transformers, fuses, switches, etc. The CEO of GE wanted to improve operational performance and create an advantage over competitors, some of which had offshored manufacturing operations to capitalize on lower wage rates. The CEO committed to no layoffs as a result of our improvement activity, and in areas where manpower needs were reduced, team members would be reallocated to different roles (with training).

At a technical and social systems' glance, GE had all the vestiges of a traditional mass production: the labor workforce was racially and ethnically diverse, but management roles were predominantly male and white, and there were not many women in production or management roles. Much of the technology and tooling used in production processes were dated, in a sort of craftsperson's job shop way. The members of management and production were generally friendly and open (yet skeptical) to the idea of an outsider coming in to help improve the organization.

The facility was large and had many different products and product lines, so GE selected a focus area to create what would be a continuous improvement model from which other teams and departments could see and learn – it was the pad-mounted gear line. Pad-mounted gears are sometimes green, brown, or gray metal boxes located just outside of residential and commercial buildings that contain electrical switches and fuses for that building. The high-level manufacturing processes for pad-mounted gears were similar to automobile manufacture: stamping and forming of the metal body, welding and grinding, painting, sub-assembling, and final assembling into a finished and saleable good. The metal body was conveyed between departments and within departments using forklifts or hand dollies. Pad-mounted gears came in a variety of applications and styles, which translated into just under 80 part numbers from which customers could choose.

The general strategy for the improvement work flowed in a similar way as kaizen trainings and problem-solving activities: clarifying the business/customer needs, selecting a focus area, grasping the initial condition, establishing a target condition and plan to achieve performance improvement results, then doing it (quickly). However straightforward this approach may sound, it tends to be deemed problematic for members who struggle with transformation (a point I will return to later).

In terms of people development, my coaching primarily targeted two members of GE's internal continuous improvement group (whose manager reported directly to the CEO), followed by production team members, supervisors, and the manager of the pad-mounted gear line. On a monthly cadence, I met with and coached GE's top management. GE would also develop me in many ways, including learning the absolute genius of electrical engineers who convert ideas into products that the benefit society.

Warning: this section dives deep into the technical systems domain to show (1) how challenging transformational improvement work can be and (2) it is good thinking to shoot for the moon, miss, but still end up among stars. As an improvement team, we studied how pad-mounted gear parts and information flowed through the production system. On a material and information flow chart, we documented the flow from incoming customer orders and raw steel to finished goods staged for shipment – shown in Figure 4.1. The material and information flow chart, perhaps more commonly known as a value stream map (see *Learning to See*, 1998), is another of Toyota's improvement tools used to tell the story of improvement in a succinct and visual way, even for the most complex of technical systems. For ease of reading, I greatly simplified the graphic, excluding details about timing, inventory quantities, and other facts required to fully understand and capture how customer demand was met.

The problems, inefficiencies, and opportunities to improve the system were summarized in the "problem" clouds. There was muda of inventory (material stagnating) between all major processes, extra handling of those materials, no standardized work, quality concerns, rework, downtime especially from part shortages, and the lead time from customer order to staging was extremely difficult, if at all possible, to accurately predict. Imagine ordering from a restaurant and the lead time to receive your order was so unpredictable that the staff could not reasonably estimate how long you would wait? For a single snapshot of lead time, we totaled the inventory

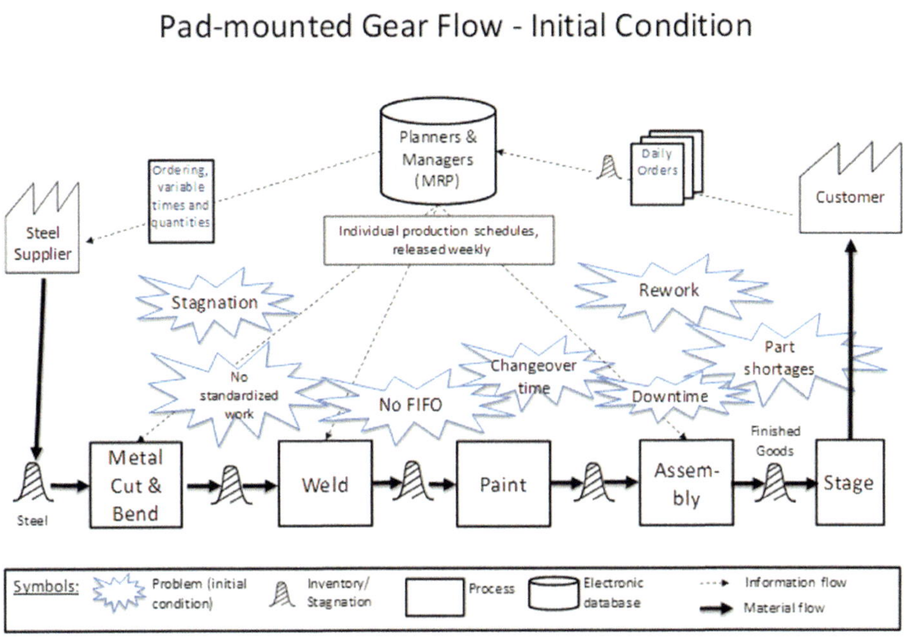

Continuous Improvement (CI) Implementation in Other Organizations ■ **65**

Pad-mounted Gear Flow - Initial Condition

Figure 4.1 **Initial material and information flow chart at a high level**

of metal bodies in the system and divided that sum by takt time to arrive at roughly 12 weeks. The material and information flow chart was a living document, continuously being updated as the team continued to observe and study the system even as we progressed to discussing what would be the ideal production system.

One of the extraordinary features of TPS thinking is that you get to imagine the ideal condition of the system. This ideation is some amalgamation of experience, vision, courage, and daring to believe in the limitless capability of your team. Figure 4.2 lays out the ideal condition for the pad-mounted gear line at GE. In essence customer orders would flow through the system in a manner that achieved the lowest possible lead time, and the inventory required to account for fluctuations in customer demand would be managed in a very particular way. This ideal condition was not too idealistic, in fact, it describes what Toyota production lines aim to achieve. However, for GE this would be a considerable stretch requiring a transformation of thinking and performance. So, let's dive into the basic thinking behind this ideal condition as most of it applies to most organizations – even those that do not make things.

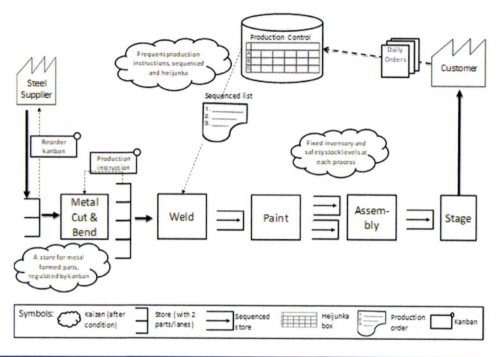

Figure 4.2   Ideal material and information flow chart for model line/area

Production Control Will Level (Heijunka) Incoming Customer Orders

In the ideal condition, the production control group would receive customer orders and level (heijunka) them over a fixed time period. Leveling may seem high effort, but this way of thinking minimizes overall burden on the system and muda, thus lowering costs. Suppose GE's planning period was bi-weekly and the volume of orders was 200 units. For a five-day work week, leveling by volume would result in 20 units per day. Suppose the variety of orders included 100 units of product A, 50 units of product B, and 50 units of a mix of low runners (called "X"). Leveling by variety would translate to 10 units of product A, 5 units of product B, and 5 units of the low runners per day in the sequence of A, B, A, X, and repeat until the daily demand was filled. See Figure 4.3.

Leveling is also important at the process level when there is variation work content for different product types. Suppose the assembly process

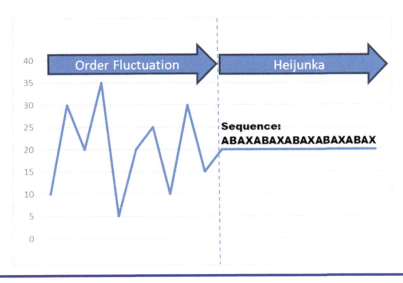

Figure 4.3 Example of leveling by volume and variety

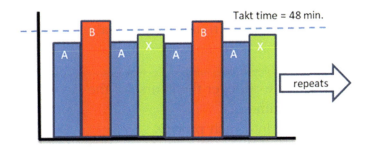

Figure 4.4 Example of leveling by work content (within a production line)

required 40 minutes of work for product A, 50 minutes of work for product B, and 40–50 minutes of work for the low runners. Leveling by work content, as in Figure 4.4, smoothed the workload to meet customer demand with less muda of wait time or additional manpower.

Pull System to Manage Production and Stores

For several reasons, mostly relating to quality and safety, GE did not maintain finished goods inventory but rather built to order. In the ideal condition, there was a build-to-order pull system in which downstream processes pulled materials (as they needed them) in sequence to reduce the accumulation of inventory or stagnation between process. Pull systems may seem like high effort, but the benefits include lead time reduction, increased coordination and collaboration among production control and internal processes, and greater visual management. So, ideally, the metal cutting process would have a (supermarket-like) store of parts with fixed minimum and maximum levels, from which customers like Weld could pull what was needed, when it was needed, and in the quantity needed, thereafter releasing a signal back to the metal cutting process to replenish the store. As for how to store inventory, there would be sequenced lanes in the stores for welding, paint, and assembly, with fixed minimum and maximum levels clearly marked and labeled, and a first-in-first-out flow. Finally, the staging process would pull parts from assembly to prepare them for the truck shipment.

Processes and Conveyance Have Standardized Work

In the ideal condition, there would be standardized work for each repetitive process and defined conveyance routes for material movement that had or allowed:

- Safe and repeatable work over the course of the day
- Pace based on takt time
- Quality checks built into each process
- Team members to signal or call for help (andon) when needed
- Periodic ergonomics evaluations
- Anyone to easily see if a team member was working ahead or behind pace
- Stability (the correct parts with good quality)

Daily Management and Living the Values

In the ideal condition there would be real-time support for production problems and good two-way communication between team members and supervisors (at all levels of management). Those responding to issues that impact the customer would do so with a sense of urgency – seeing the customer as a patient on the operating table so all hands on deck. Also, there would also be visual tracking of key performance indicators, especially safety, quality, and customer demand fulfillment, so management can easily see abnormal conditions and take action to remedy issues.

The other part of transformation work to consider and plan for was the social systems, which was just as critical to achieving enduring high performance. I mentioned the transformational values and principles at Toyota included:

- Improvement thinking: kaizen and problem-solving with urgency, data, challenge, learning, reflection
- Disciplined way: standardization, perseverance
- Teamwork thinking: respect, humility, autonomy, flexibility, competition
- Communication way: frequent, succinct, visual

Also, Toyota's bar for leaders living the company's values was very high – and the basis for TMC-Japan leaders scolding or walking out on management members who showed poor leadership thinking. Ideally, in GE's transformation work, management would absorb and share these values and develop their kaizen capability so they can better support and develop the rest of the organization.

As for GE's values and principles, what mattered most was the members' lived reality, which as an outsider could be discovered through observations, discussions, and asking why. I gathered that the social context at GE was quite traditional with old-school manufacturing ways and dis-eased interactions between management and labor. Therefore, it was extremely important as we journeyed through that we did so with integrity – meaning little to no division between our words and actions with production team members and our physical shopfloor changes. In other words, if we were shooting for theideal in technical systems architecture, then we also had to shoot for the ideal in the social milieu – including treating production members as owners of processes and with the highest level of respect. There were a few explicit conversations in this area, but for the most part, I endeavored to lead by example in this way throughout thier transformation journey.

From Ideal to Just-Do-It

Having laid out the ideal condition for the sake of a mental roadmap of the overall technical and social systems improvement, GE's improvement team established and agreed to specific targets and a schedule for shopfloor transformation, starting with stability and standardization at assembly and staging processes. In TSSC, we typcially created challenging implementation schedules knowing that the level of self-awareness required for an individual (and certainly an organization) to accurately predict the timing of their own transformation is usually too high. More often than not for me (and other TSSC coaches), the original plan and schedule of activities were not met and required constant revision. By the way, the same was true for Toyota; for example, while problem-solving (jishuken) activities were time-boxed, there was no guarantee that each member and team would learn enough about the system to get performance improvement results in that week. Learning is one of those unknowns that come along with such a journey, and I tend to believe it happens when it is supposed to happen, no sooner, no later – even though it can be influenced with good coaching. And unlike a traditional consultant who does the work of implementation (without transformation) and thus can more reliably predict timing, my mission was to teach them "to fish," to believe in themselves, and to always imagine the ideal so that they would continuously strive for performance improvement and operational excellence.

For assembly and staging improvement, we started with the implementation of standardized work and the struggle was real. After some classroom-to-shopfloor training on the concepts, the improvement team grasped the initial condition for each of the assembly processes using the standardized work documentation tools discussed in the Chapter 1 and Appendix. The discipline required to study the nuance and details of production work was equal parts frustrating and confusing to some improvement team members, who thought it was a waste of time and not their responsibility. The negative emotions GE members would experience, I had already experienced early in my TPS journey. Like my mentors and as their coach, I showed them by example, allowed them to try their own way (and fail), and at times released the tension of the challenge. This meant doing some of the work myself until their "Aha" moment happened and the improvement team members (and production team members) saw with their own eyes the benefits. They persevered and eventually got through it.

The total processing time to make one unit of the most frequently produced part was roughly 3 hours – sometimes produced with five team members (a skeleton crew) or nine team members (a full crew). By the way, this is not the intention of manpower flexibility as it more desirable to design a smooth and consistent pace throughout the shift and days of the week. The number of assembly processes in the target condition after kaizen and standardized work implementation was determined by dividing the total processing time for a pad-mounted gear by dividing the total

Continuous Improvement (CI) Implementation in Other Organizations ▪ **71**

by takt time. GE spent weeks deciding if the takt time calculation would be based on two shifts (their normal) or one resulting in a 40-minute per unit pace versus a 20-minute pace. Because this decision significantly impacted some team members' work–life balance, it was necessary for team members and management to take time to deliberate. A 40-minute takt time would be equivalent to a Toyota production team member trained in 40 different processes, compared to the typical four or five. The point is that standardized work was a big effort for both kaizen activities and also training team members to the standard. The team agreed to trial a 20-minute takt time to move forward with creating standardized work for each process, after which they trained the production team members on the new process and posted the documents lineside.

The team and I spent most of our time on the shopfloor either studying the system or implementing changes. Every moment the improvement team spent in production, they invested in the social domain establishing greater trust and collaboration with production members. They placed a whiteboard in the area for production team members to write the concerns and challenges they experienced throughout the day. As the improvement team worked hard to standardize processes and address those concerns, I could clearly see a difference in team member relations as production team members saw the new system benefiting them. On the other hand, the improvement team became overburdened with the volume of issues and concerns to remedy on top of completing standardization implementation.

Over the course of many months, the improvement team implemented several changes that supported standardized work:

- Set up a visual pacing mechanism for the line so team members and management could see allocated time per unit
- Located parts and tools line side at the process to reduce team member walking and searching for tools
- Dedicated conveyance team members to supply the line with the necessary parts (prior, the team members left the line to find and get parts)
- Installed andon lights at each process on the line to call for assistance in real time
- Created two team leader roles, the most experienced and knowledgeable members, to respond to andon calls (prior to the team leader, each member had to figure out their problems on their own)
- Tracked actual production versus planned output on an hourly tracking board (could clearly see ahead and behind conditions)

72 ■ *Toyota's Improvement Thinking from the Inside*

- Visually marked the floor, walls, etc. to help show normal from abnormal conditions within the process
- Created an ergonomic evaluation system to measure burden (as members were more exposed to repetition burden in the paced system)
- Created a cross-training plan for all team members

Also, to remedy the overburden and reduce the perception of chaos within the improvement team, we temporarily split members into one of three focus groups: (1) model area problem-solving group – addressing poor quality and missing parts; (2) standardized work implementation group – addressing best work methods and standardized work updates; and (3) pull system group – addressing conveyance and parts storage issues. This triad approach led to investigation and improvement work in the following areas:

- Changeover time reduction activities at upstream processes
- Part fit problems with design engineers
- Ergonomic improvements with health and safety and maintenance
- Relocation of subassembly processes next to assembly to reduce part shortages and delivery
- Introduction of total productive maintenance (TPM) to maintain team

Problem-Solving

Once there was sufficient understanding of standardized work and buy-in from the production members, the assembly line began to flow, and most team members preferred the new way. With this new system, the next level of struggle began – problems like missing parts or tools or poor part fit that were normally hidden or ignored became more noticeable. In coaching the improvement team to act quickly to solve team members' problems, it became apparent that there was a lack of experience in production problem-solving. There were more problems surfacing than people and time available to address them, members did not know how to solve problems with a sense of urgency, and root cause analyses and countermeasures were rare. To develop this skill, the organization invested in classroom-to-shopfloor problem-solving training for some of the production members and other staff who were available to support the model area transformation. As I mentioned previously, root cause problem-solving is a powerful skill that supports enduring high performance, but it takes time to develop. It also takes a strong sense of organizational teamwork such that when a given problem traces back to another department, those members are willing to help and take action. This was another area to develop over time at GE, as we were met with skepticism when investigating problems outside of the model area.

Results

Shooting for the ideal condition was (and is) a sure-fire way to make performance improvements, even if the team falls short of hitting actual targets. By the conclusion of my time with GE, the transformation work toward ideal was still in its infancy but already had measurable and anecdotal results, which included a 25% productivity improvement, 30% reduction in floor space and lead time for assembly, greater teamworking, more predictable work for team members, improved ergonomics management, greater problem-solving capability, and greater trust by team members that problems raised would be addressed. Some production team members received pay raises as a result of the higher output coupled with greater skill development.

Reflections

The results, while promising, were a mere splinter of the actual capability of the improvement team and organization if they continue to develop transformational values. Given the cultural context, their collective pace of learning was very typical as well as how they cycled through the stages of transformation (denial, frustration, bargaining, overwhelm, and acceptance) for each distinct improvement activity (e.g., standardized work, problem-solving, daily management). Some of the resistance from the improvement team, specifically, was rooted in their prior understanding of conventional "lean" practices, which focus solely on the technical systems domain, not the social domain nor how significant was personal development on the journey. At the conclusion of my transformation work with GE, the improvement team reflected on our journey and their remarks nod to the gaps in the social systems domain of the transformation model:

74 ■ Toyota's Improvement Thinking from the Inside

- We did not know what type of kaizen people were required (improvement thinking)
- We did not react quickly enough when we were not getting the results we expected (improvement thinking)
- We did not solve problems in such a way that they didn't reoccur, only 40 out of 800 problems had root causes addressed (improvement thinking)
- As leaders, we could have done a better job coaching, selecting, and motivating (improvement thinking)
- Training in standardized work took considerably longer than we thought because we did not plan at a detailed enough level (discipline way)
- Supervision did not take ownership of daily management of KPIs (teamwork/improvement thinking)
- We did not reach agreement with production on one shift or two (teamwork thinking)
- We did not ask assembly line supervision enough questions about how we can help. We added to their burden as we improved the line, giving them new tasks to support like getting parts (teamwork thinking)
- We did not get commitment from engineering (design problems open for five months or more) (teamwork thinking)
- TSSC was not active in our planning activities (teamwork/communication way)
- We did not clearly lay out expectations, have a motivated team, or verify team members understood the concepts (communication way)

Turning to the stages of grief and transformation, a typical response is to attribute problems and delays to a lack of specificity in planning. Take, for example, another reflection point from GE, "There was too much role ambiguity between GE leadership and TSSC during visits which made it difficult to direct activities, set targets, and understand ownership for homework." I mentioned earlier that the general strategy for improvement work was simple – clarify the business/customer needs, select a focus area, grasp the initial condition, establish a target condition, and plan to achieve performance improvement results, then do it (quickly). Some specificity is part of defining the targets and target condition; however, if the planning time drastically increases for the sake of greater specificity, and at the expense of implementation time, when at the core is learning whose pace is difficult to predict, that's likely time wasted. If there is any place to assign "blame" or

Continuous Improvement (CI) Implementation in Other Organizations ■ 75

cause for delays, it is most likely somewhere between deeply studying and understanding the system (which requires discipline) and countermeasure activity (which requires creativity). This work is often difficult and uncertain, especially at the beginning. For this reason, Toyota keeps a low ratio of members to coaches in order to intensify the speed and depth of learning. In the Eastern tradition it is believed that accepting uncertainty unlocks creativity and innovation. So, if your organization has started this transformation journey and the schedules have not been met but team members are demonstrating learning and some results, be very encouraged. If there has been a struggle to get results and meet the plan, it may be a good idea to problem-solve your strategy and/or process with the transformation framework in mind.

Chapter 5

CI Implementation in Healthcare and Education

While in TSSC, I was assigned to a healthcare organization located in Boston, Massachusetts, to support operational improvements like patient flow, quality, cost reductions, etc. I was enthusiastic to apply TPS thinking into a healthcare system, but weeks into the engagement I had a change of heart. I questioned if the level of hubris among the executive who managed the engagement and some others would conflict with Toyota's way of development. Once I overheard a conversation between the executive and a high-level clinical manager who articulated he found it offensive that their prestigious hospital would engage with a car company to help them improve. This would be the only time I requested TSSC end an engagement, and my TMC-Japan boss had agreed based on how significant was leadership's commitment to the learning (and transformation) journey. I would, however, go on to work with other hospitals and eventually land an internal consultant role at a hospital where I could develop TPS thinking as an insider.

While working in healthcare, I heard over and over again from staff, "Yes, that system works at Toyota, but we don't make cars or things." So, using the transformation model as a lens, the purpose of this section is to share insights into the world of continuous improvement transformation at a healthcare institution, deep diving into one specific improvement journey that – spoiler alert – did not result in sustainable system improvements, but still there were many take-aways to learn from the experience. Let's first

76   DOI: 10.4324/9781003540670-5

begin with a crash course of how the buzz of continuous improvement in the automotive sector and manufacturing spread its way to healthcare systems.

Contemporary View of Improvement in Healthcare

As a researcher who is also engaged in civics and community, I have an affinity for scholarship that benchmarks performance within an industry and subsequently shakes up and breaks up an outdated way of thinking to usher in transformation that positively impacts our lives. Two such works in healthcare included *To Err Is Human: Building a Safer Health System* (1999) and *Crossing the Quality Chasm* (2001). In these two publications, the Institute of Medicine (IOM) called out the need for safety and quality improvement in healthcare based on evidence that medical errors and mistakes in healthcare resulted in tens of thousands of fatalities each year. The IOM also suggested that errors were not a result of bad people working in a good system but rather good people working in bad systems – systems that needed to be redesigned with safety and overall healthcare delivered at the forefront.

To support organizational development, some healthcare organizations turned to industry titans to study their methods for improvement, including TPS (and lean thinking). Some healthcare organizations had achieved notable results such as Virginia Mason Medical Center, who after two years of lean implementation reported $9 million in cost avoidance in addition to other productivity improvements, inventory reductions and savings, and lead time and set-up time reductions. ThedaCare was another exemplar story of TPS application in healthcare, reporting $10 million per year cost avoidance from productivity gains, namely, through weeklong kaizen activities (Miller, 2005). What was notable in both cases was top management's, including the CEO and board members, buy-in to the adoption of improvement thinking and tools..

For many, it may be too far a leap to see how the technical tools of TPS would transfer to and benefit healthcare. So, years later the Institute for Healthcare Improvement developed a model for improvement (Langley et al., 2009) that would address how to problem-solve poor quality and other performance outcomes such as patient/family experience, productivity, lead time, cost, etc. Their improvement approach was adopted by some

78 ■ Toyota's Improvement Thinking from the Inside

healthcare organizations including the hospital in which I worked. Sharing some of Toyota's eight-step problem-solving thinking and borrowing from the work of statistician Edward Deming, the IHI model for improvement had distinct language and features, namely:

1. Plan an improvement initiative that includes a theory, aim, plan of action, and supporting team members
2. Develop, test, and pilot changes using plan–do–study–act cycles and using statistical charts to identify special causes
3. Implement successful interventions, sustain the change, and control the system
4. Spread the change throughout the extended system

Today, there is still much work to do in spreading the improvement gospel in healthcare in such a way that brings transformation and enduring high performance. A 2021 report published by the Commonwealth Fund found the U.S. healthcare system ranked last among the top 11 high-income countries in five performance categories: access to care, care process, administrative efficiency, equity, and healthcare outcomes (Schneider et al., 2021). This was despite the fact that the United States spent the largest percentage of the GDP on healthcare. The other countries included Australia, Canada, France, Germany, Netherlands, New Zealand, Norway, Sweden, Switzerland, and United Kingdom.

Traditional Hospital Culture and the Transformational Values

The hospital was a nationally ranked non-profit pediatric academic center for both patient care and scientific research. There were many units of business or lines of care (e.g., emergency department, in-patient units, outpatient clinics, support services, and more) that for the most part operated independently, making it difficult to describe its culture – but there was no question that from new employee orientation and beyond, good patient care was the single most important and unifying mission.

At an initial glance, the hospital looked like it had traditional ways of thinking. Most members of the hospital were female, while the C-suite (CEO,

CFO, COO, CIO) and other top management positions were predominantly occupied by males. There was a considerable amount of racial diversity across the organization; however, service roles such as housekeeping, food services, and transport were predominantly occupied by people of color. The hospital had not committed to a no-lay-off policy when rolling out their improvement strategy, which could be problematic as members may choose not to engage in improvement work if they believe it will result in headcount reductions. Like many organizations, the opportunities to reduce muda (waste) abounded in extra and expired inventory, patient flow and experience, resource scheduling and manpower allocation, records manag-ment, billing, etc. One of the first and most striking differences compared to a TPS setting was the volume of management meetings and how rarely they were structured to clarify operational goals and advance toward them.

Another cultural nuance in healthcare that negatively impacts quality is the prestige effect, in which team members fear speaking up to or overly rely on the prestigious member to ensure quality. There have been situa-tions, for example, in which a patient had surgery on the wrong body part, or the wrong surgical procedure, or in some cases it was altogether the wrong patient and no one on the surgical team intervened. These events are rare but should never happen so recognizing this risk the hospital instituted the "time-out" rule, a planned stop in the surgical process when every mem-ber of the operation room team (e.g., surgical technicians, nurses, surgeon fellows, etc.) stops to individually and verbally confirm quality, specifically the right patient, right procedure, right location. Time-out implementation was a significant accomplishment, but there were many more ways in which the prestige effect could compromise the performance improvement journey.

Recognizing the need for transformational change and responding to IHI's call to action to improve patient outcomes and experience and reduce costs, the hospital endeavored to learn how to best accomplish thier mission. The history and journey of improvement at the hospital began several years prior to my arrival as they had already committed to becoming a leader in healthcare continuous improvement, adopted the Institute for Healthcare Improvement's improvement approach, and made investments in the organi-zational structure and way of working some of which included:

- The creation of an improvement department (similar to TEMA's OMDD), whose head reported directly to the CEO, staffed with improvement coaches, data analysts (who mined big-data from the IT system), translational researchers (who provided evidence-based best care practices), and others

- The creation of several curriculums with classes in improvement theory, statistics, and a practicum
- The development of a five-year strategic vision and yearly improvement goals that aimed to link efforts of individual units into common organizational goals
- Daily team meetings (called huddles) in several clinical areas to improve communication, especially between cross-functional areas and groups

In my early explorations of the hospital learning, coaching, and offering my support for improvement work in both clinical and non-clinical spaces, I saw a variety of improvement projects that demonstrated the organization was on its way to mastery of IHI's improvement methodology in a similar way that some organizations develop six-sigma belts. I saw fearless leaders who believed in the possibility of continuous improvement and tirelessly worked to instill transformational values (e.g., improvement thinking, a disciplined way, teamwork thinking, and the communication way) toward cultural change. On the surface, the hospital was doing all the right things to transform from traditional thinking and peformance levels to enduring high performance - but there were gaps I noticed once I engaged with shopfloor improvement efforts.

Clarify the Business/Customer Need

As I interacted with members and project teams for improvement work, most people were open to the idea of change yet with a healthy dose of skepticism – no different from my personal journey. One of my first team-based improvement projects was supporting and coaching the neurosurgery value stream. What prompted the improvement work was an anesthesiologist, who had worked hundreds of neurosurgical cases, recognized significant differences in the time it took to complete a neurosurgery case depending on who was on the operating room (OR) surgical team. She saw the fluctuation in case time as waste (muda) and was passionate about improving the system so she discussed the idea with a couple of the neurosurgeons on staff. They agreed that by reducing waste in the process, patients would have less exposure time in the OR, the surgeons could possibly see more patients in a day (increased capacity), and the amount of time a patient had to wait for a scheduled surgery could be reduced - all wins. The anesthesiologist led

Grasp the Initial Condition

(and sponsored) an improvement team that included me (as an improvement coach), the anesthesiologist, two neurosurgeons, a data analyst (also serving as improvement coach), an operations manager, and considerable participation and support from the surgical technologists, nurses, and others.

Grasp the Initial Condition

To start, I knew very little of the surgical process, a humble brag as I considered myself and my family lucky to never have required major surgery. That said, learning what actually happened in the operating room was unlike any other work experience or process study – the miracle and genius of that level of science, engineering, and practice was nothing short of amazing. It was deeply humbling study for me – as for the surgical team, it was routine patient care. Our improvement team spent weeks on the floor observing and meeting with members who directly impacted operating room capacity and patient flow: the schedulers, registration staff, perioperative nurses and staff, sterile processing team members, surgical technologists, OR nurses, surgeons, anesthetist nurses, physicians, and others. It was a complex technical system based on the number of separate systems, work groups, user preferences, dynamic adjustments required for unpredictable emergent cases - on top of the typical operational management challenges of absenteeism, equipment failure, poor quality materials, etc.

We developed a patient and information flow chart (a modified MIFC) to show the initial condition for patient flow from hospital entry through exit of post-anesthesia; see Figure 5.1. The basic process flow for scheduling patients for surgery involved multiple groups including the surgeons and their schedulers and the OR business managers who used multiple electronic data management systems (such as EPIC) to determine the case length and required OR time. As the surgery date approached, the coordinating groups included the neurosurgery staff, the sterile material and supplies group, nursing staff, and central OR schedulers who assigned the specific operating room, peri-operative and OR staff – all using electronic data management systems. Finally, when the patient arrived for the surgery, they were registered, consulted by a variety of physicians, rolled into the OR for the procedure, rolled into the post-anesthesia care room, then sent to an in-patient room for observation and care. In between those high-level steps, there was muda of patient wait time and fluctuation in times for a variety of causes. There was not much standardization of work processes (as defined by TPS)

82 ■ *Toyota's Improvement Thinking from the Inside*

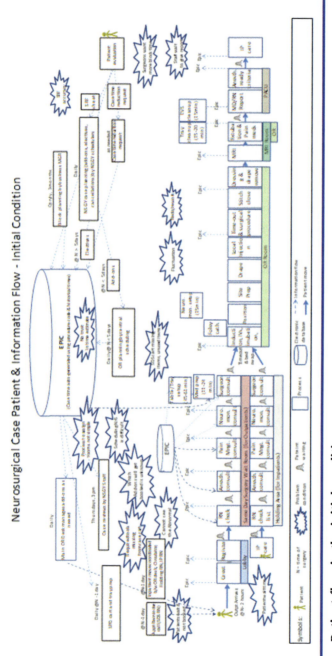

Figure 5.1 Patient flow in the initial condition

from scheduling to post-operative care as members performed work in their own way based on their training and experience. The lead time from patient registration to OR entry was just over two hours. The lead time in the OR suite ranged from 4.5 to 11 hours, which included a variety of procedures and surgeons. Our improvement team data analyst attempted to compare the data we captured to what appeared in the EPIC system to verify they matched. This was no simple task because there were multiple databases to mine and strange codes that had to be interpreted. A direct data comparison was difficult so the observations we made were the most reliable. It is also important to note the management gap - there was no owner of lead time or OR capacity as a KPI, no visualization of it, no targets for it, and no expectation to improve it over time.

The complexity of the system created burden for many members. For example, it was difficult for the scheduling group to allocate OR time efficiently, surgeons did not always receive the right supplies at the right time, sterile processing department members struggled to supply each surgeon with unique materials and supplies, and the list went on as every group that touches patient flow had legitimate concerns. Such complexity tends to compound and hide problems that might otherwised be quickly solved to improve patient flow and customer satisfaction (the customer being the next downstream processing group in total patient care).

Ideal Condition and Plan

Ideally, we could simplify the system so that routine work processes and the process of improvement were not overly burdensome. Our improvement team's heads were spinning with all the nuance of the system, which also included regulatory requirements (e.g. training, documentation, procedural tasks, etc.) in the background of our improvement work. So, what would simple look like in terms of True North? Figure 5.2 shows the ideal patient flow.

Ideally, patients would be scheduled using heijunka (leveling) thinking, which would mean staying as close as possible to the first patient in (consultation), first patient out (placed on the schedule) while also considering the volume and mix of case types. So, for example, if the fixed scheduling window is one week, in any given week the cases are sequenced to level the daily burden on the staff as well as the number of patients seen per day.

84 ■ *Toyota's Improvement Thinking from the Inside*

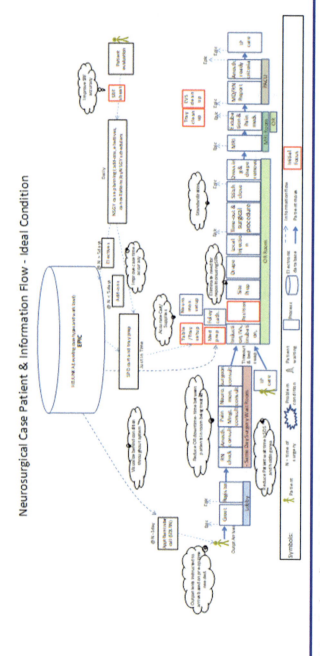

Figure 5.2 Patient flow in the ideal condition; reduction in muda (waste) and lead time

Also, the OR would have delivery of the right materials, in the right amount, at the right time from the sterile materials supply group and from stock rooms.

To ensure good leveling, the actual work content (and timing) for each case type and OR team member would be required. In TPS, we would use work measurement tools (such as the standardized work analysis sheets and yamazumi charts) to study, improve, and establish work elements and times for each process. Additionally, since this was a teaching hospital and physicians and others were trained during procedures, we would study the variation to determine how to adjust standard processing times. Once the standard was implemented, we would track major deviations (or fluctuations) and problem-solve to get back to standard.

The ideal system would also include quality conditions and checkpoints within and between processes – such as the time-out process, in which all members of the OR team stopped to confirm the right patient, right procedure, right location. The nature and number of quality checks would be based on actual problems experienced in practice. Another key characteristic of the work processes would be for each member (and process) to easily see abnormal from normal conditions, and in the case of an abnormal condition, there would be someone to help problem-solve with urgency as a part of the daily management routine. In TPS, this role is filled by the team leader and group leader who are not tied to a specific process.

This ideal condition would be a journey that required deep study, commitment, and long-term thinking and planning as it would be transformational. It would also require a cultural shift in which management members are not afraid to show operational performance levels such as patient lead time, quality, safety, experience, cost, etc. And, as with most transformations, it would be difficult to predict the timing considering the numbers of unknowns like learning pace.

Just-Do-It and Results

If the journey of a thousand miles begins with a single step, the improvement team was off to a practical start. We prioritized improvements within the patient flow process that would get quick wins, namely, more efficient turnover of the operating room once the patient exited, reduction in the fluctuation of process times within the OR, and reduced over-processing and rework in the OR. After six months, the results included a 59% reduction in OR changeover and setup time from 69 minutes to 28 minutes and a 23% reduction in OR time (for the most frequent case type). This was achieved by identifying work steps that could be performed outside of the OR and performing those steps sooner or later, reducing non-value-added work steps performed inside of the OR such as repositioning the patient and improving the communication and coordination of activities between the OR team members and housekeeping services. As much as those wins did energize the team, they were not necessarily sustainable, neither was there a measurable impact to overall OR capacity. This achievement gap was in part attributed to our failure to standardize and spread the improvements to other work shifts and neurosurgical teams.

Reflections

If I could reverse engineer the ecosystem with the ideal patient care in mind, I would design the organizational structure to support improvement of the entire neurosurgical value stream with a leader responsible for lead time, quality, and other key performance indicators. As it stood, the organization just like the improvement team itself had cross-functional members with leadership for each function (e.g., surgical technicians, nurses, physicians, scheduling, housekeeping, etc.) that did not necessarily collaborate or manage in the way of continuous and transformational improvement, so if an improvement project fizzled out without substantive improvement or member learning, it was of no consequence. Sponsorship of improvement work is no replacement for ownership and people/process development.

In Toyota there is a principle of kaizen referred to as "inch wide and mile deep" - if you must choose between the two it is better to go mile deep for greater growth and performance over time. Failures and frustruation are natural parts of transformation work and deep learning, but there was no demonstrable frustration on our improvement team's journey from having tried and failed and tried and failed. Quite the opposite, members on the team remained consistently pleasant and politically correct. Many of my observations of improvement work at the hospital were inch deep and mile wide, perhaps due to the prestige effect and general reluctance to challenge members. If so, that comes at the cost of members (and the organization) not being stretched to their full potential in the high calling of patient care.

Standardization

I hearken back to the transformational value of a disciplined way and that standardization should be non-negotiable for ensuring stability, reliability, quality, low cost, etc. and should be continuously and emphatically preached and demonstrated by leadership. Our improvement team members (and beyond) associated standardization with a loss of autonomy and saw it unfit for that particular work environment; it may have even conjured the mental image of healthcare team members as programmable robots. Quite the opposite, high-reliability work teams and organizations harness the part of us that is wired for habits (good or bad) and routines. For example, in my observation of the "all-star" team neurosurgical cases, I noticed the surgeon used the same strokes of the wrist when prepping the patient with iodine, the nurse placed the catheter with very little fluctuation in time, the anesthesiologist intubated with the same sequence of steps, and many other examples. These were good starting points for sharing best practices and implementing standardized work so that members across shifts and operating rooms maintain the highest level of reliability for patient care.

To show proof of concept, in another part of the hospital an improvement team trialed standardized work in the use of respiratory equipment, specifically, the high frequency oscillatory ventilator, which supports patient lung function. The standardized work elements were determined based on the experience of practitioners as well as the equipment manufacturer operating manual. The level of detail in the breakdown of work into elements was negotiable and ultimately determined through trial and error with the level of specificity sufficient for a new trainee to follow the work instructions correctly. The team's final version of the standardized work instructions consisted of 80 elemental work steps to operate the equipment. The results of implementation showed promising results in terms of ease of training and, of course, safe operation of the equipment. Small steps toward ideal.

CI Implementation in Education

As my first child approached school age, I began researching local elementary schools and learned that our public neighborhood school was classified as failing by the state's standards, in large part based on standardized test performance starting from the third grade. I reached out to my mom-group, a bunch of moms I had met at story time at our local library who were equally concerned about school quality and choices. They led me to good options in our district's magnet school lottery system. Our family was fortunate to be selected to attend a well-rated and regarded magnet school – although my heart broke for our friends whose kiddos were not chosen and, in general, for the parents who want quality school choices but lack access. Another option was private school, and the state did offer vouchers to subsidize the cost; however, my siblings and I were all publicly schooled in K–12, so that was my default preference. Also, and perhaps more importantly, I personally believe that public education is critically important for creating a more equitable, just, and safe society, and it was this core belief that took me on a journey of improvement within educational systems, and my first target was our low-performing neighborhood school.

The purpose of this section is to share my deep dive experience with continuous improvement in education, which was as much technical as it was personal. Again, spoiler alert, the work did not result in organizational or system-level improvements, although there were good results from which to learn and continue to make change. Let's first begin with the application of TPS brand of continuous improvement in education.

A Framework for Quality Improvement in Education

I have a large family with many educators and when we discuss topics like "school reform" or improvement, most of us have such strong opinions it can be as divisive a topic as politics and religion. My affinity for the TPS improvement way is not intended to discount all the hard work and past efforts to improve educational quality and outcomes, but rather to build upon it with a common organizational transformation framework. The popularity of continuous improvement in education has grown somewhat, but it is far from proliferated, and certainly, it lags behind the healthcare sector's unified focus on quality and adoption of model for improvement. The good news is that there lies an opportunity to learn from the healthcare movement especially since educational and healthcare systems share similarities from a performance outcomes point of view. Both have quality outcomes highly influenced by the end customer (e.g., the students and the patients), and both systems tend to be highly bureaucratic and complex, which can make transformation seem like an insurmountable task. I believe the Institute of Medicine's interpretation of the healthcare quality chasm directly applies to education: *incidences of poor quality are way too prevalent in education and poor quality is not a result of bad people but rather good people working in bad systems – systems that need to be re-designed with quality and overall education delivery at the forefront.*

From the research of poor quality in healthcare emerged a framework for healthcare improvement. So, is there a model or framework for improvement in education? Two authors from the RAND research institute suggested the Malcolm Baldridge National Quality Award for organizations in education, business, healthcare, and other non-profits as a good framework feducational performance excellence (Stecher & Kirby, 2004). Established in 1987 and managed by the US National Institute of Standards and Technology, the Baldridge criteria highlight various aspects of the TPS that directly support a culture of continuous improvement, including:

- Customer and market focus: how the organization determines requirements and expectations of customers and markets
- Process management: how key production and delivery and support processes are designed, managed, and improved
- Human resource (HR) focus: how the organization enables its workforce to develop its full potential and how the workforce is aligned with the organization's objectives
- Leadership: how senior leadership guides the organization and practices good citizenship in public
- Strategic planning: how the organization sets strategic directions and determines key action plans
- Data and analytics: how the organization manages, uses, and analyzes data and information to support key organizational processes and the organization's performance management system
- Results: how the organization performs in customer satisfaction, financials, HR, supplier and partner performance, and operations and how the organization performs relative to competitors

There have been educational organizations that journeyed into the world of continuous improvement and achieved measurable performance improvement. For example, academician William Balzer (2010; 2016) investigated continuous improvement efforts at several colleges and universities that had implemented TPS tools and methods. The improvement activities ranged from quality improvement in classroom instruction to performance improvements in operations such as payroll, hiring, and facility work order management that resulted in significant yearly cost reductions. This is promising considering the exorbitantly high and still rising cost of higher education.

Cost reductions are beneficial for educational organizations as well as the families and communities that fund them. However, if you live in a low-performing K–12 neighborhood like we did, then quality and performance improvement are higher priorities. Such performance gaps in education are, I believe, some of the biggest opportunities for continuous improvement practice and research. Although this work is relatively new in education, some organizations have demonstrated various levels of success. For example, the Learning Enterprise Institute (see LEI.org), a non-profit organization started by "lean thinking" pioneer James Womack (Womack et al, 1990) worked with K–12 educational organizations to help transform a high-cost and underperforming school to a nationally recognized higher performing school. Also, during my time in Toyota Production System Support Center (TSSC), we had an engagement with a public high school in Rhode Island, which sought guidance and coaching on how to improve student retention. After the one-year TSSC-led activity, there was a 50% reduction in the student drop-out rate. That partnership ended abruptly amid disputes between district leadership and the union. As I mentioned, K–12 education reform initiatives can be quite divisive and perhaps for no other reason than continuous improvement transformation efforts might be lumped into "flavor of the month" initiatives without gravitas.

Continuous Improvement Thinking Applied in K–12 Education

To transform our low-performing neighborhood elementary school, I turned to my own children. First, I enrolled my youngest child in their preschool class so I could closely engage with the community of teachers, staff, parents, etc. I met with the school principal that summer to explain my professional background and offer my support for any improvement work that had already been underway. Her enthusiasm was initially high and we agreed to start on performance improvement efforts at the beginning of the school year. Anticipating that we would need parents/caregivers to participate in the improvement activity, we first surveyed the teachers to collect their perception of parent/caregiver involvement levels. There was no active parent organization at the school so I simultaneously worked with the school resource coordinator to help establish one. I also joined the school's eight-member decision-making committee as a parent representative. Finally, at the district level I joined a separate parent group formed by an active school board member who created the group as a mechanism for good two-way communication with parents across the district.

After several meetings with the school principal and vice principal, we landed on specific performance measures, standardized test scores (both math and reading), and the pilot area was one of three fourth-grade classes. To lead the deep learning on our improvement journey they chose a highly regarded fourth-grade teacher. I was confident that our improvement work would be successful based on the vice principal's palpable excitement during our initial meetings. The next step included understanding the pilot fourth-grade's performance gap - followed by target setting, and root cause problem solving. However, we never made it to discussions of the data as a group. Instead, the school and lead teacher jumped right to countermeasure (or intervention) implementation based on their assumptions. It was like pulling teeth to coach the improvement group back to more deeply understanding the performance gap. Then, just like that, time was no longer on our side, and our improvement work for that academic year ended with no results and the improvement team left in the denial stage of transformation.

When I could predict that the learning journey at the low-performing school would not be successful, I turned to my oldest child to dive deeper into and learn more about the standardized test and improvement. She was a second grader at a higher performing magnet school in the same district and with the same standardized test and protocol. I met with her teacher to explain my objective and gain her support for the effort. The process of improvement with my daughter served as my ideal version of how I had hoped the learning journey played out at our neighborhood school. I should note that before this deep dive, I paid little attention to the details of my children's standardized testing in large part because I did not have much access to the computer-based exams administered at the school, neither had her teacher raised any performance concerns during our past conferences.

Clarify the Gap

The school district had three standardized test periods per academic year. The initial diagnostic test occurred in September (roughly five weeks into their academic year), followed by a mid-year diagnostic in December, then a final diagnostic in May. The improvement work with my daughter began eight weeks prior to the final standardized test, and I focused on math only because she consistently exceeded the proficiency targets in reading. Figure 5.3 shows her overall performance and gap to the target for the most recent

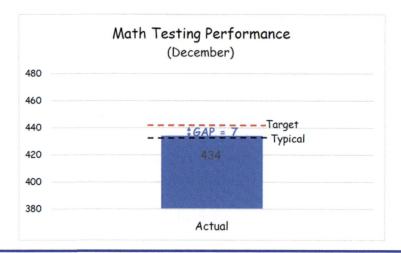

Figure 5.3 Math testing performance versus target (and typical) scores in December

(December) diagnostic period. She scored 434 points, which was 1 point above the statistically "typical" student, but 7 points shy of the target, 441. The next step was breaking down the seven-point gap.

Break Down the Problem

While computer-based testing made scoring much more efficient compared to the days of paper exams, it made breaking down the gap (for parents and teachers) more difficult because the actual data and scoring logic were not clear or accessible. This made root cause problem-solving more difficult and hopefully gets resolved with better transparency with standardized testing. So, I had to rely on the computer-generated analytics, which was automatically outputted for each student and made available through the teacher's online account. The teacher provided me with a printout of the analytics for my child's mid-year diagnostic performance, which helped to relatively break down the performance gap across four learning domains:

- Numbers and operations – concepts included counting, base-ten number system, adding, subtracting, etc.
- Algebraic thinking – concepts included skip-counting, fact-families, using equations to solve addition and subtraction problems, etc.
- Measurement and data – concepts included counting money, measuring length, telling time, picture graphs, etc.
- Geometry – concepts included two- and three-dimensional shapes, geometric terms, partitioning, etc.

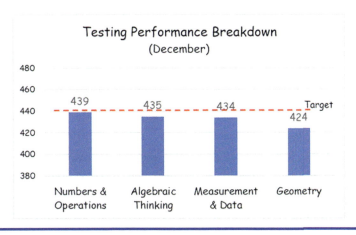

Figure 5.4 Breakdown of performance gap by math domain in December

Figure 5.4 shows the gap for each domain. According to the teacher, the magnitude of each domain gap correlated to the length of time she covered the topic in class. In other words, by December more class time was spent on numbers, operations, and algebraic thinking, and very little time was spent on geometry, which would be covered in upcoming lessons.

While it was helpful to see the performance gaps by domain, in the absence of each exam question and scoring, it was not possible to precisely break down the numerical gaps or see specific performance deficiencies. In lieu of the actual exam questions, I settled for her classroom assignments that were sent home (and accumulated in a storage box throughout the academic year) to better understand the gap. An assumption I made, which could justifiably be challenged even in my own mind, was that the standardized test sufficiently correlated with the classroom assignments. Over the course of two weeks, I went through her old in-class math assignments, which mostly included the first three learning domains and little geometry, which matched the teacher's feedback. I checked for errors and incorrect responses to see if any themes emerged in the math concepts – no obvious themes emerged. Then, over the course of several days we sat and reviewed the incorrect responses so I could observe how she worked through them and get real-time feedback from her. She understood most of the content and chocked most of her errors up to "mistakes" with no real understanding of why. I verified that a knowledge gap was not the issue by retesting her using similar questions with different numbers. She also indicated that sometimes she felt that she did not have enough time to complete the work.

Target Setting and Root Cause

Ideally, with this study and improvement work, the entire 7-point performance gap would close. The only facts to go on that helped explain the performance gap was my daughter's feedback. So, if mistakes and time constraints in combination truly accounted for most of the errors on her assignments and the standardized test questions, then my thought was at the root of the problem lied distractions from the external environment and mental distractions from fatigue, boredom, sleepiness, and/or stress. I had already witnessed the extent to which distractions could affect her performance, especially during our year of compulsory virtual schooling during the height of the COVID-19 pandemic.

This level of analysis surpassed my training and understanding, so I phoned a friend, a school psychologist in the district, hoping to arrive at a quick and practical way to measure the underlying sources of distraction and how they linked to mistakes. We were not able to arrive at a good measurement way, so in order to progress, I settled on a "shotgun countermeasure" approach, which is, in the absence of a precise cause-and-effect relationship, to aim in the general area of the cause/problem and the dispersion of the shotgun countermeasures should be effective at eliminating the problem.

Countermeasure

So, the countermeasures were aimed at the broad category of distractions. There was not much I could do to eliminate external distractions such as talking and the plethora of typical fourth-grade behaviors in the classroom, but I could try to minimize their impact by developing my daughter's ability to perform well in their presence. This same thinking also applied to mental distractions. My thoughts on countermeasures were twofold: improvement of her mental focus and greater content mastery to improve her speed. Also, the countermeasures were designed to be effective but to avoid overburden or development of anxieties around math. In the six weeks leading up to the final standardized testing period, the countermeasures included the following:

- For mental focus and stress reduction
  - increased strictness of bedtime
  - increased our yoga practices at home
- For greater content mastery and time on task reduction
  - practiced problems at home with time limits – performed randomly

- teacher assigned extra practice assignments online and by paper – maximum time of 30 minutes per week
- applied more math concepts in her home life (e.g., asked her for the time using only analog clocks, let her pay for small store items, let her measure in cups while I cooked, asked her to measure things in house using rulers and tape measure) – performed randomly
- reviewed errors made on classroom assignments – ongoing, one problem per day as assignments came home
- coached her on reviewing her work before submitting it

Results

Overall, the countermeasures as a whole seemed to be effective, although my daughter admitted that she did not review her work before submitting her test responses. Her results on the third and final standardized test in math are shown in Figure 5.5. She improved her overall score by 8 points from the previous test period, exceeding the district target by a single point. She showed the greatest improvement in the algebraic thinking domain, 4.8% higher, followed by the measurement and data and geometry domains. There was no improvement in the numbers and operations domain, and the geometry domain still showed the greatest opportunity for improvement – best explained by the lack of coverage in class and at-home practice assignments.

In TPS, success is measured in the learning as much as in the results, and I learned more than I had anticipated in the deep dive with standardized testing. For all the assumptions I made without validation, either because I lacked access to parts of the system (e.g., the actual exam questions and scoring logic) or had limited understanding of the psychology of distraction,

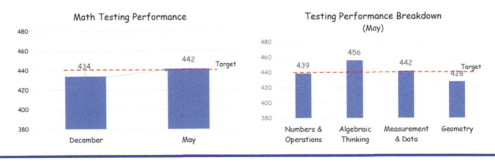

Figure 5.5 **Results on final standardized testing period**

Yokoten (Spread) the Results

I took those learnings, including a better understanding of the bureaucracy of the school system, to a third-grade class at our magnet school. I had the same objective as our neighborhood school, to discover what was in the performance gap and what could be done quickly and at low cost to help close the gap. I met with a third-grade teacher, explained my professional background. In the post-COVID era of significant student performance drops, she was enthusiastic to work together. A key difference between engagement at this school compared to the neighborhood school was my intentionality in spending time in the classroom to directly observe students, and the improvement results were significant and positive.

After several meetings and discussions, the teacher chose reading standardized test performance for the improvement focus. This was an impactful choice as the state and school had a third-grade reading guarantee in which students were required to pass one of two standardized tests in reading in order to move on to fourth grade (with some exceptions). The magnet school had a history of high academic performance and took the reading guarantee seriously.

At the start of the improvement work, I met with the entire class in small groups of four to six, for 20-minute sessions, to build a positive relationship with the class and get a general sense of their capability. The teacher allowed the students to leave the classroom for each session. We practiced reading fluency, decoding, comprehension, and other grade-3-level skills that were part of the curriculum. The initial standardized test diagnostic was administered in September. Figure 5.6 shows student performance for the class of 23 students, whose scores averaged 185 points. Once the teacher and I reviewed the data we narrowed the focus and attention to the students whose performance was below the proficiency target (of 195 points) and below the average of 185.

There were eight students in this focus group, two of which were eventually excluded because they received academic support from the school also outside of classroom time. The teacher provided me with supplementary assignments for the focus group members to practice reading fluency (speed and accuracy), comprehension, recall, and inference in individual 15-minute

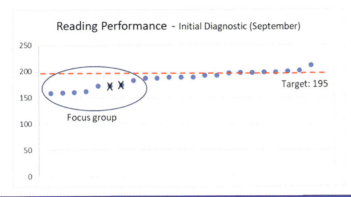

Figure 5.6 **Results of the first standardized test – each blue dot is a student score**

sessions each week. The second standardized test diagnostic was administered in December and all but 5 students in the class met the 195 proficiency target, including one from the focus group and the two receiving academic support. The increase in performance average was 9.4% for the focus group compared to 6.8% for remaining class. The student in the focus group that met the proficiency target of 195 in December no longer met with me.

To prepare the remaining five students for the final standardized test, each one was given tailored practice work based on the teacher's capability assessment and guidance, which ranged from sight word review (basic) to comprehension and inference (higher level). Also, because we had fewer students in the focus group, the time I spent with each increased to 18 minutes during our weekly session. I also attempted to reach out to the parents/caregivers of the focus group members to discuss the improvement work, our goals, and understand what if any additional home support was needed. Because of the district's privacy policy, the school could not give me the family's contact information, so I sent notes home with the focus group students as well as communicated through the teacher. Only two of the five families responded to me via phone calls. We talked through the performance gap, goals, and suggestions for improvement. I also offered encouragement and my support outside of school hours if needed – neither of them requested any additional support from me.

The third and final standardized test diagnostic was administered in April - the performance results are shown in Figure 5.7. Twenty of the twenty-three students (87.0%) met or exceeded the proficiency target score of 195 in one or more of the three testing periods. The average performance improvement over the academic school year was 15.9% for the focus group members compared to 9% for the others. The three students who did not meet the

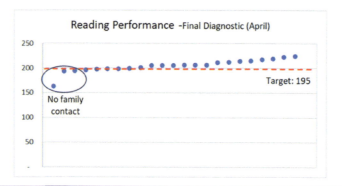

Figure 5.7 Final standardized test results – each blue dot is a student score

proficiency target were the focus group members whose families I failed to engage, demonstrating the critical role family engagement plays in K–12 education, especially for improvement work.

We also examined how the class reading proficiency results compared to others during the same academic year. Figure 5.8 compares the percentage of third graders who met the reading proficiency target in the pilot class (87.0%), the magnet school's third-grade overall (69.1%), the district (47.5%), and the state (62.3%). The pilot class demonstrated significantly higher performance.

At the conclusion of the work, we discussed the results with school leadership who would decide on how to spread the thinking in order to continuously improve across grades and over time. While I was hopeful, I was not expecting a broad and sweeping change in such a bureaucratic system as public education. I had already experienced the many layers of resistance to

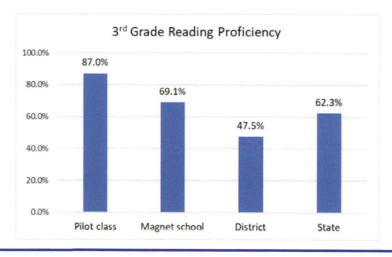

Figure 5.8 Reading proficiency comparisons

change working with parents, teachers, administrators, and the board at our neighborhood school. It was clear that no one person or group had ownership over educational quality. Hopefully, this story serves as a motivation for anyone on the frontline of education (teachers, parents, and others) that there is an improvement way that may have started in industry but is effective and accessible to all – even if the bureaucracy of the organization and system has massive inertial forces that prevent change. No pun intended, the key to continuous improvement in educational systems, as well as others, is to keep learning and persevering.

Conclusion

This book is probably much denser than I intended it to be, and if so, let me apologize for that. My aim was to make the transformational gift I had been given clearer and more accessible for everyone and every organization to inspire a confidence and audacity to continuously improve. From a Toyota philosophical point of view, people have a tendency to hide problems (not surface them) and continuous improvement does not happen naturally. So, starting from new member onboarding, the company is very deliberate about developing team members' thinking way and capability to see muda (waste) and work quickly to reduce it and improve operational performance. In terms of organizational structure, Toyota maintains small groups of highly trained TPS coaches across the enterprise whose duty is to do and coach improvement.

Like any high-performance environment not everyone makes it, which is to say, able to overcome the challenge(s) to get to the other side toward transformation. One way of thinking about the evolution to high performance is the transformation model presented in this book. It conceptualizes the alignment of technical tools for improvement, organizational values and principles around improvement, and a spirituality or mindset that allows members to endure challenges and losses and to tap into a higher purpose – from which innovation and creativity emerge to help achieve enduring high performance. I am a witness that this transformation journey requires sacrifice especially by leaders, but pays off with high dividends. Fitness guru Billy Blanks in his bootcamp work-out series would repeat "you have to lose yourself in order to gain [strength and endurance]." This is true of organization fitness as well. These concepts are rarely mentioned in the books, articles, and conversations about the lean enterprise, high reliability organization, and total quality management but are nonetheless critical to learning and achieving high performance.

102 ■ *Conclusion*

I have not spent much time discussing specific management or leadership roles and expectations in the transformation journey in part because in TPS culture it is a given that a key role of leaders is to develop self as well as his/her members. A transformation journey outside of a Toyota culture, however, may necessitate a greater prescription of roles and expectations in aligning the three domains of the transformation model. Whether inside or outside of Toyota, the journey of pursuing perfection, the ideal condition, or continuous improvement is just plain difficult and typically full of more perceived failures than successes. However, over time the individuals and organizations that develop the right thinking will see results in superior operational performance, less muda, and ultimately deliver greater value for the customers, patients, students, and/or the community they serve.

Appendix

Chapter 1

Chapter 1 – The following standardized work analysis tools are foundational for the thinking and method of work improvement and thus have been described in detail.

Time Measurement Sheet

The time measurement sheet is used to grasp basic information about the process and is the basis for the other standardized work documents. Before measuring time, it is important to observe the process and understand the purpose of work, the work sequence, and the parts/materials/tools required. Job rotation is prevalent across Toyota production facilities, so to the question of who to observe, it should be the most experienced team member (if it matters). Also, most production processes have a primary process owner who can verify the standardized work steps. As a best practice, observe multiple team members to identify nuances, knacks, and burden that team members have.

Because there are so many technical details, I provided a non-manufacturing example, bagel preparation, to demonstrate the use of the time measurement sheet – see Figure A.1. This simple process cycle starts with getting a bagel and ends with placing the finished product on a plate.

The basic steps to capture time measurement data include:

- Observe 10 cycles of the process to understand the work
- **Element and starting point** – break the process into work elements, each with a starting point that can be an identifiable action or sound
- **Observations** – with a stopwatch, record element times for ten observed cycles, including any periodic work (which is work that happens periodically such as changing out empty totes)

103

104 ■ Appendix

Time Measurement Sheet

| Dept: | Group: | Team Member: | | | | Date: | | | | | Qty/Shift: | | |
| Process: | | Recorder: | | | | Shift: | | | | | Takt Time: | | |

#	Element	Starting Point	Observations										Lowest Repeatable Time (LR)	Fluctuation (Range)	Adjusted Element Time
			1	2	3	4	5	6	7	8	9	10			
1	Get bagel half	Reach for bag	3.3	3.9	3.8	3.8	4.0	4.1	3.6	3.4	3.4	3.4	3.3	0.8	3.3
	Walk	Release bag	1.3	1.2	1.1	1.4	1.0	1.7	1.1	1.3	1.5	1.3	1.0	0.7	1.0
2	Add butter	Reach for knife	3.5	3.2	3.2	3.2	3.2	2.7	3.0	3.1	3.0	3.0	2.7	0.8	2.7
	Walk	Release knife	1.6	2.0	1.3	1.3	1.5	1.6	2.0	2.0	1.4	1.3	1.3	0.7	1.3
3	Microwave (6 secs)	Reach for Mic.	9.9	8.8	9.0	9.4	9.0	9.4	9.8	9.7	9.5	9.5	8.8	1.1	9.8
	Walk	Mic. door close	1.7	2.0	2.0	1.9	1.9	1.6	1.8	2.0	1.7	1.7	1.6	0.4	1.6
4	Inspect and plate	Stop walk	2.7	2.9	2.6	2.4	2.4	2.5	2.5	2.7	2.8	2.4	2.4	0.5	2.9
	Walk	Release plate	2.2	2.2	2.6	2.0	2.1	2.1	2.0	2.4	2.5	2.0	2.0	0.6	2.0
	Total Element Cycle Time		26.2	26.2	25.6	25.4	25.1	25.7	25.8	26.6	25.8	24.6	23.1		24.6

Periodic Work (p/w)	Element #	1	2	3	4	5	6	7	8	9	10
Wipe microwave plate				3.3							
(every 10 cycles)											

Adjustments: The 1.5 second difference is added to elements #3 (1.0 seconds) and #4 (0.5 seconds).

Element Cycle Time Totals		Total Cycle Time Measurement (cycle time + periodic work)									
Minimum: 24.6		1	2	3	4	5	6	7	8	9	10	Lowest
Fluctuation (not include. p/w): 2.0		26.2	26.2	28.9	25.4	25.1	25.7	25.8	26.6	25.8	24.6	24.6
Average: 25.7												

Figure A.1 Time measurement sheet

- Any waiting by the team member should be documented. In the bagel example, the person waits 6 seconds each cycle for the microwave to complete
- Walking, while it takes time and should be documented, is not considered a work element
- **Lowest repeatable time** – determine the lowest repeatable time by taking the minimum (time) of the 10 cycles – even if the lowest time was observed only once – which is 3.3 seconds for element #1 because this represents the best time that could be repeatable (or normally) performed
- **(Element) fluctuation** – compute the fluctuation for each element and walk by taking the difference between the lowest and highest observed times – 0.8 seconds for element #1. To clarify, Toyota refers to unplanned time differences between cycles as fluctuation and planned differences due to part/product design as variation
- **Total element cycle time** – sum the element times for each cycle to get the total element time for each observation – which ranges from 24.6 seconds to 26.6 seconds. Circle the lowest total – this is the **process cycle time**, 24.6 seconds in the tenth observation

- **(Cycle time) fluctuation** – of the ten observations, take the difference between the highest and lowest total element cycle times, 2.0 seconds (= 26.6 seconds minus 24.6 seconds). This difference is used on the work balance chart
- **Periodic work** – for each cycle observation, add any observed periodic work time to the total element cycle time to compute the total cycle time measurement
- **Lowest repeatable sum** – sum the lowest repeatable element times, 23.1 seconds
- **Adjusted element time** – take the difference between the process cycle time (which is the lowest observed cycle) and the total lowest repeatable sum; add this difference or portions thereof to one or more elements. For any elements not adjusted, transfer the lowest repeatable time to the adjusted element time column. Sum the adjusted element times, which should equal the lowest observed cycle time. For example, the difference between the lowest cycle time (24.6 seconds) and the total lowest repeatable time (23.1 seconds) is 1.5 seconds. This 1.5 second difference then gets added back to any of the elements, in this case elements #3 and #4, to adjust their element times to 9.8 seconds and 2.9 seconds, respectively. How to determine which elements to adjust? The answer should be based on logical factors such as highest fluctuation, highest element time, and/or elements that contain inspection work
- The adjusted element times are used for the remaining standardized work documents

Standardized Work Combination Table

The purpose of the standardized work combination table is to quickly show/ see muda in the timing and interaction between the production team member and the machine/equipment time. The work element, machine (auto), and walk times are taken from the time measurement sheet. Figure A.2 shows a standardized work combination table using the bagel food prep example. On the left-hand side, the work is described, and the right-hand side, there is a visual depiction of the progression of processing time versus takt time. Wait time (for the microwave) is highlighted as a problem (with a red arrow), and if the cycle time were not the same as takt time, that would also be highlighted as a problem.

This example highlights the quantity component of standardized work. To create a smooth workflow, the process needs one piece of standard

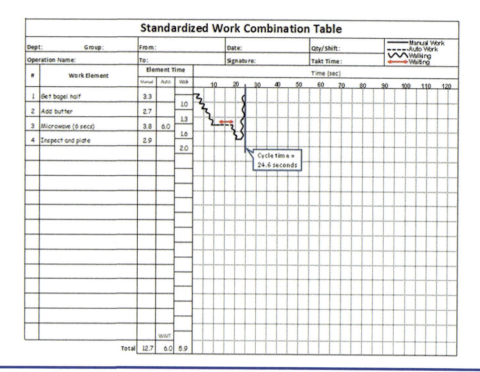

Figure A.2 Bagel food prep standardized work combination table

in-process stock so that the person will no longer wait idle while the microwave completes. With this kaizen, when she unloads the microwave with the finished piece from the previous cycle, she can load and start the piece from the current cycle and eliminate 6 seconds of wait time, shown in Figure A.3. This simple kaizen would increase productivity over 24%.

Standardized work chart. The purpose of the standardized work chart is to quickly show/see muda in the layout of the process. Again, the work element, machine (auto), and walk times are taken from the time measurement sheet. Figure A.4 shows the standardized work chart using the bagel food prep example (before any kaizen). On the left-hand side, the work elements, walk times, and machine times are listed. On the right-hand side is the simple layout of the workspace with blocks used to show where the hands of the team members interact with the parts/materials. A couple points for the standardized work chart:

- Manual work and walk are depicted where the team member's feet rest and travel
- The icons used to indicate safety or quality concerns and standard in process stock level should appear inside of the process boxes such as the quality point in element #4.

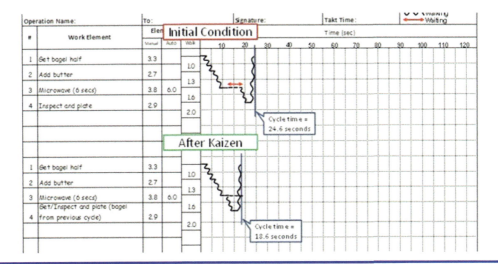

Figure A.3 Bagel food prep standardized work combination table with before and after kaizen

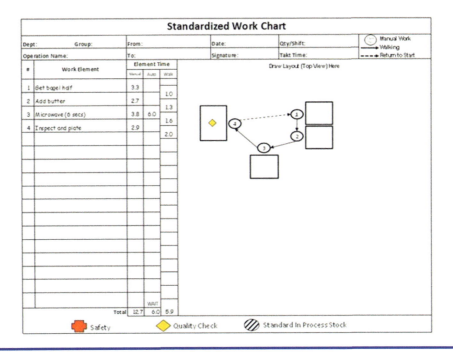

Figure A.4 Bagel food prep standardized work chart

Standardized Work Chart, Moving Line

The moving line chart shown in Figure A.5 differs from the standardized work chart in the graphical area, which is designed to capture the team members' work steps while traveling on the moving conveyor with the

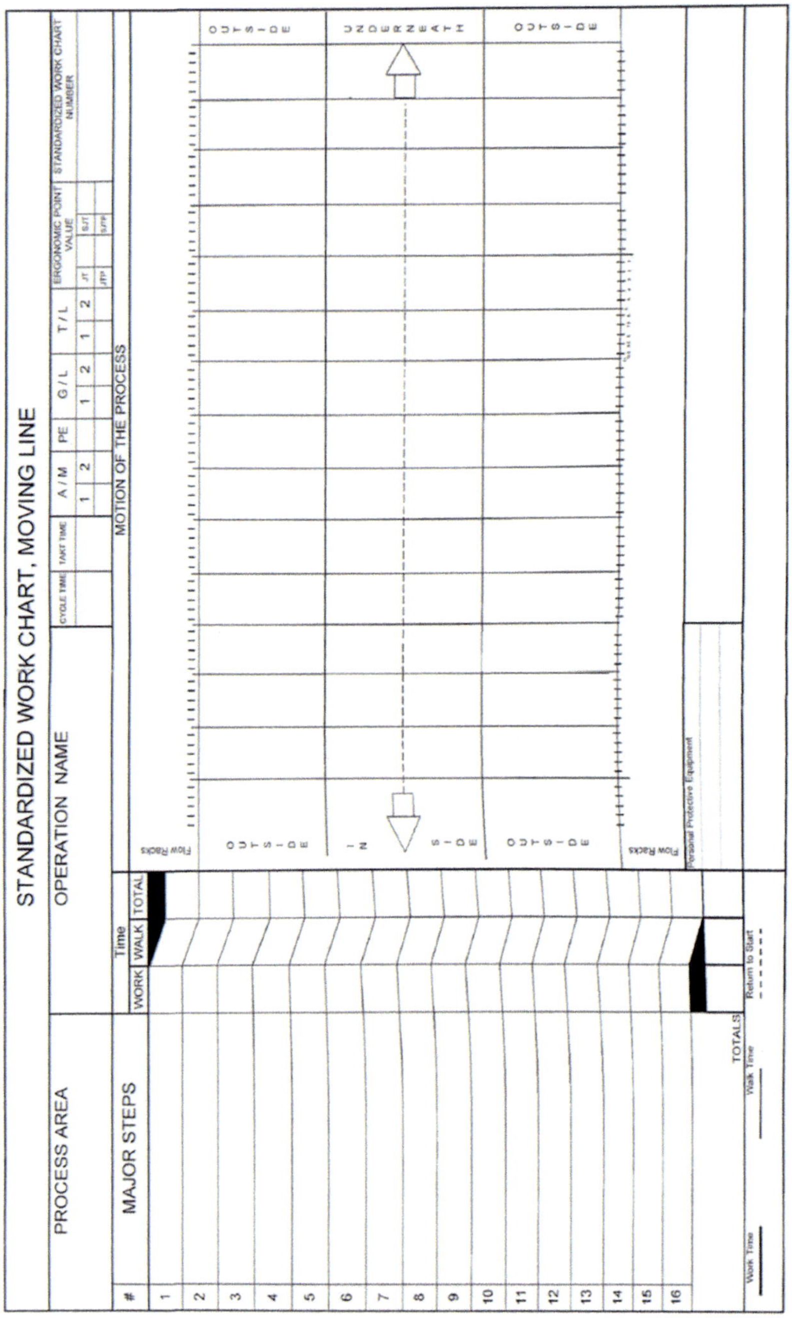

Figure A.5 Standardized work chart for a continuously moving production line

vehicle. Typically, the assembly parts were stored in a fixed location, off the conveyor. Most importantly, this tool is used to visualize dynamic problems, such as the muda of walking and waiting caused by interference between team members (e.g., someone working on the rear of the downstream vehicle blocking the path of someone working on the front of the upstream vehicle). This tool was also used to show muda accumulating over time due to model and cycle time variations (e.g., a high cycle time model followed by another high cycle time resulting in team members getting behind or two low cycle time models back to back resulting in wait time).

Machine Capacity Sheet

The machine capacity sheet is used to analyze and show if machine capacity can meet customer demand. Capacity is based on the process's manual work time (i.e., loading, unloading, starting machine), the machine's cycle time, and changeover time. Figure A.6 shows generic example machine capacity calculations for a production line with two injection molding machines.

Based on time studies of injection mold machines #1 and #2, the manual time to load/unload the machine plus auto time to cycle through a part totals 18.5 seconds and 27.6 seconds, respectively. The changeover time, also based on time studies, is 59 seconds (for an interval of every 100 units) and 66 seconds (for an interval of every 200 units). With these data, the capacity of each machine can be calculated by the following equation:

Machine Capacity Sheet										Name:
Dept:	Group:	Part #:		Part Name:			Demand:		Date:	
#	Process Name	Machine No.	Basic Operation Time			Tool Changes		Capacity (967)	Remarks: Manual ____ Auto ------	
			Manual Time (s)	Auto Time (s)	Time to Complete (s)	Interval	Time Required (s)			
1	Injection Mold #1	IM001	3.0	15.5	18.5	100	59	1414	3s⊢⊣ 15.5s	
2	Injection Mold #2	IM002	2.5	25.1	27.6	200	66	967	25s⊢⊣ 25.1s	

Figure A.6   Machine capacity sheet example

110 ■ *Appendix*

$$\text{Capacity per shift} = \frac{\text{Available time per shift}}{\text{Time to complete a unit} + \left(\dfrac{\text{Tool change time required}}{\text{Interval}}\right)}$$

In the example of injection mold #1:

$$\text{Capacity per shift} = \frac{\dfrac{7.5\text{hr}}{\text{shift}} * \dfrac{3600\text{sec}}{\text{hr}}}{18.5\text{sec} + \left(\dfrac{59\text{sec}}{100}\right)} = 1414 \, (\text{rounded down})$$

The overall capacity of the manufacturing cell is the minimum of all computed capacities, which in the above example is 967 units per shift. If this capacity does not meet demand, then there must be a kaizen focus to improve output through a machine cycle (auto) time, manual time, and/or changeover time reduction(s).

Work Balance Chart

The next standardized work kaizen tool is the work balance chart (also referred to as yamazumi), whose purpose is to visualize the condition of the process(es), specifically, process cycle time, fluctuation, periodic work time, changeover time, and cycle time average, and quickly see how it compares to line speed and takt time. With the exception of line speed and takt time, the work balance chart data are taken directly from the time measurement sheet. The line speed can be captured by direct observation (if someone tells you the line speed, trust but verify with your own eyes).

Figure A.7 shows an example of a work balance chart (with a single process) excluding actual values. From this visual tool, one can quickly show/ see problems and muda with the process and set kaizen targets:

■ On average, the cycle time is greater than the line speed, which likely results in disruptions to subsequent/downstream processes, a need for overtime, and/or the team member must rush to catch up. These conditions are no good and thus should be the prioritized kaizen opportunity
■ Fluctuation, or time differences from cycle to cycle, is problematic because it raises the average time, may cause a team member to fall

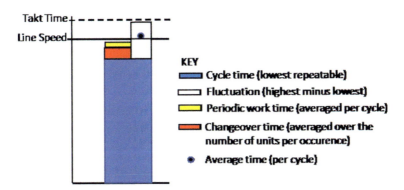

Figure A.7 Work balance chart (single process)

behind, and hides muda. Fluctuation is often a signal of team member burden, so deeply understanding the causes to kaizen is also a priority
- The gap between cycle time and takt time will lead to wait time that is often hidden, which shows this is a kaizen opportunity

The work balance chart is also used to visualize the condition (including muda) of an entire line or work group and set a kaizen target for the line. Figure A.8 shows an example of a work balance chart with seven processes (excluding actual values) before any kaizen. This number of processes to target after kaizen is determined by adding the cycle times for the seven processes (referred to as sigma CT or ΣCT) and dividing the sum by takt time (Figure A.9).

$$\text{\# Processes} = \Sigma CT/\text{takt time}$$

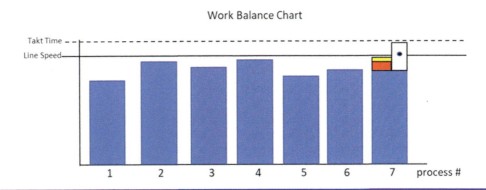

Figure A.8 Work balance chart for a group or line

If, for example, the sum of the seven cycle times was 336 seconds and takt time was 60 seconds, then the number of processes to target through kaizen would be 5.6, which would round up to 6 processes (or round down to 5 but with more aggressive kaizen strategy).

Chapter 1 – Calculating sample size using the statistical t-distribution (Niebel & Freivalds, 2003):

* Observations are assumed to be normally distributed. However, since the sample size was small, a t-distrubution applies and

$$\text{sample size} \left[\frac{(\text{t-value} * \text{sample standard deviation})^2}{(\text{error probability\%} * \text{sample})} \right]$$

In the case of a sample of ten cycle time observations, with a 55-second mean, 2.97-second standard deviation, .05 error probability %, and t-value of 2.262 (based on 9 degrees of freedom),

sample size = 6 observations required

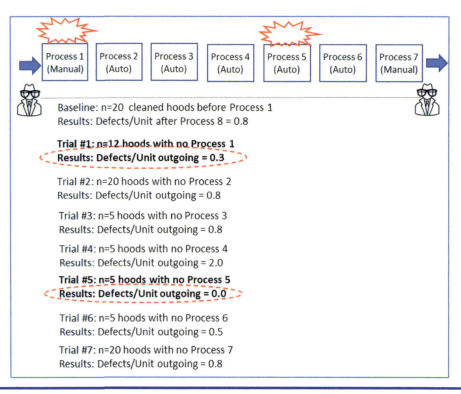

Figure A.9 The results of the seven trials in problem-solving defects per unit in the primer process. Processes #1 and #5 had a significant drop in defects per unit when the process was "turned off"

References

ACGIH. (2005). *Hand Activity Level, Two Thousand Five TLV for Chemical Substances and Physical Agents and Biological Exposure Limits.* Cincinnati: American Conference for Governmental Industrial Hygienists.

Balzer, W. K. (2010). *Lean Higher Education: Increasing the Value and Performance of University Processes.* New York: CRC Press.

Balzer, W. K., Francis, D. E., Krehbiel, T. C., & Shea, N. (2016). A review and perspective on lean in higher education. *Quality Assurance in Education: An International Perspective,* 24(4), 442–462.

Barnes, R. (1980). *Motion and Time Study: Design and Measurement of Work.* New York: Wiley.

Committee on Quality of Health Care in America & IOM. (2001). *Crossing the Quality Chasm: A New Health System for the 21st Century.* Washington, DC: National Academy Press.

Dinero, D. (2005). *Training Within Industry: The Foundation of Lean.* New York: Productivity Press.

Gilbreth, F. B. (1911). *Motion Study, A Method for Increasing the Efficiency of the Workman.* New York: D. Van Nostrand Company.

Langley, G. J., Moen, R. D., Nolan, K. M., Nolan, T. W., Norman, C. L., & Provost, L. P. (2009). *The Improvement Guide* (2nd ed.). San Francisco: Jossey-Bass.

Liker, J., & Franz, J. (2011). *The Toyota Way to Continuous Improvement: Linking Strategy and Operational Excellence to Achieve Superior Performance.* New York: McGraw-Hill.

Liker, J., & Hoseus, M. (2008). *Toyota Culture: The Heart and Soul of the Toyota Way.* New York: McGraw-Hill.

Liker, J., & Meier, D. (2006). *The Toyota Way Field Book.* New York: McGraw-Hill.

McAtamney, L., & Corlett, E. N. (1993). RULA: A survey method for the investigation of work-related upper limb disorders. *Applied Ergonomics,* 24, 91–99.

Miller, D. (2005). *Going Lean in Health Care.* IHI Innovation Series white paper. Cambridge, MA: Institute for Healthcare Improvement. Based on presentations by J. Womack, A. Byrne, O. Flume, G. Kaplan, J. Toussaint.

114 ■ References

Moore, J. S., & Garg, A. (1995). The strain index: A proposed method to analyze jobs for risk of distal upper extremity disorders. *American Industrial Hygiene Association Journal*, 56(5), 443–458.

Niebel, B. W., & Freivalds, A. (2003). *Methods Standards and Work Design*. New York: McGraw-Hill, chapter 9.

Ohno, T. (1988). *Toyota Production System Beyond Large Scale Production*. New York: Productivity Press.

Rother, M., & Harris, R. (2001). *Creating Continuous Flow*. Brooklin, MA: Lean Enterprise Institute.

Rother, M., Shook, J., & Lean Enterprise Institute. (1998). *Learning to See: Value Stream Mapping to Create Value and Eliminate Muda*. Brookline, MA: Lean Enterprise Institute.

Schneider, E. C., Shah, A., Doty, M. M., Tikkanen, R., Fields, K., & Williams, R. D. (2021, August). *Mirror, Mirror 2021—Reflecting Poorly: HealthCare in the U.S. Compared to Other High-Income Countries*. New York: Commonwealth Fund. www. https://www.commonwealthfund.org/ publications/fund-reports/2021/ aug/mirror-mirror-2021-reflecting-poorly

Shook, J. (2008). *Managing to Learn*. Boston: Lean Enterprise Institute.

Spear, S. (2004, May). Learning to lead at Toyota. *Harvard Business Review*, 82(5), 78–86.

Spear, S., & Bowen, H. (1999, September–October). Kent, decoding the DNA of the Toyota production system. *Harvard Business Review*, 77, 96–106.

Stecher, B. M., Kirby, S. N., & Rand Education (Institute). (2004). *Organizational Improvement and Accountability: Lessons for Education from Other Sectors*. Santa Monica, CA: Rand Corp.

Taylor, F. W. (1911). *The Principles of Scientific Management*. New York: Harper & Bros.

Womack, J. P., Jones, D. T., & Roos, D. (1990). *The Machine that Changed the World*. New York: HarperPerennial.

Index

A3, 13–14, 28, 39, 45, 59, 60
Automatic loom, 24
Automation with human sensing, 23–24
   deep fryer with automated alerts, 25
   in fast-food operations, 25
     Sakichi Toyoda's innovations, 24
   soda dispense, 25
Automotive paint processes, 43
Autonomy, 3, 37, 39, 69, 87
Autonomy, kaizen trials, 6

Balzer, William, 89
Burden, 6, 10–13, 24, 29, 45, 72, 74, 83
Burden reduction, 10, 13, 24, 29
   physical burden, 12
   safety/ergonomic considerations, 9

Coaching style, 4, 7, 16, 19, 38
Communication way, 37, 39, 40, 69, 74, 80
Continuous flow, 25–26
Continuous improvement (CI)
     implementation, 63–66
   educational organizations, *see*
     Educational organizations, CI
     implementation
   healthcare organizations, *see* Healthcare
     organizations, CI implementation
   manufacturing sector, *see* Manufacturing
     sector, CI implementation
Continuous improvement model, 63–66
Countermeasure evaluation matrix, 57
Cultural immersion, 1, 15
Culture, Toyota, 1, 16, 33, 102

communication, 39–40
discipline, 38
improvement thinking, 37–38
organization structure, 35–37
teamwork, 38–39
Western vs. Eastern regions, 40
work setting, 34
Cycle time, 5, 12, 104–105
   fluctuation in, 5, 13

Deming, Edward, 33
Disciplined way, 37, 69
Double consciousness, 14–15

Educational organizations, CI
     implementation, 88
   cost reductions, 89
   K–12 education, 90–91
     breaking down performance gap,
       92–93
     clarifying performance gap, 91–92
     countermeasure, 94–95
     results, 95–96
     root cause, 94
     shotgun countermeasure
       approach, 94
     target setting, 94
Engine subassembly line, 2, 6
Ergonomics, 9, 13, 29, 68, 73

Fishbone diagram, 54
Focus groups, 72
Five whys (5-why's), 54, 55

116 ▪ *Index*

Gemba (value-added work location), 4, 43, 46, 86

Guiding Electric (GE), 63

Healthcare organizations, CI implementation, 77
  business/customer need, 80–81
  contemporary view, 77–78
  ideal patient flow, 83–85
  IHI model, 79–90, 80
  initial patient flow, 81–83
  reflections, 86
  results, 95–96
  traditional hospital culture, 78–80
  transformational values, 69
Heijunka, 16, 22, 27, 66, 83
High frequency oscillatory ventilator (HFOV), 87
High-level manufacturing processes, 63

Improvement thinking, 37
Initial condition analysis, 12
Institute for Healthcare Improvement (IHI) model, 77, 79, 80

Jidoka, 22–25
Jishuken (self-learning) activity, 44–46
Just-in-Time (JIT), 25

Kaizen activity, 2, 11, 36, 45, 53
Kaizen (improvement), 30
  definition of, 30
  eliminate muda, 30
  standardization, 30
Kaizen training, 2
  autonomy, 3
  collaboration, 6
  definition, 2
  documenting and analyzing, 4
  focus area (muda, ergonomics, cycle time), 12
  group trials, 3
  innovation in kaizen, 12
  kaizen trials, 6, 12
  line balancing, 3
  maintenance team contributions, 6, 12
  productivity improvement, 6

standardized work chart, 4
training activities, 3
Key performance indicators (KPIs), 43
  sub-KPI vs. main KPI, 53
Kiichiro Toyota, 25
K–12 education, 90–91
  breaking down performance gap, 92–93
  clarifying performance gap, 91–92
  countermeasure, 94–95
  results, 95–96
  root cause, 94
  shotgun countermeasure approach, 94
  target setting, 94

Lead time, 20, 22, 23, 25, 46, 64, 65, 67, 73, 77, 83–86

Machine capacity sheet, 109–110
Managing to Learn (Shook), 39, 59
Manufacturing sector, CI implementation, 63
  conveyance routes, 68
  focus groups, 72
  ideal material and information flow chart, 66–67
  improvement team's standardization, 71–73
  initial material and information flow chart, 65–66
  leveling by volume and variety, 66, 67
  leveling by work content, 67
  problem-solving, 72–73
  production control, 66–67
  pull system, 67–68
  reflections, 73–75
  results, 73
  technical systems, 16
  transformational principles, 69
  transformational values, 69
Material and information flow chart, 64, 65–66
Material shortages, 23
Muda (waste), 2, 3, 5, 12, 23, 29, 30, 40, 47, 64, 66, 67, 84
Muscle memory, 14

Nemawashi (iterative, planning), 2, 45, 61
New United Motor Manufacturing (NUMMI), 28

Ohno, Taiichi, 7, 26, 30–31, 34
OMDD, *see* Operations Management and
 Development Division (OMDD)
Operations Management and Development
 Division (OMDD), 1, 15–16, 46
Operations Management Consulting
 Division (OMMD), 34

Pad-mounted gears, 63
Paint shop process, 43
 automotive paint processes, 43
 conveyor process, 43
 countermeasure evaluation matrix, 56–57
 countermeasure schedule, 57
 crater defects, off-lined vehicles, 48
 crater defects, paint layer, 51
 fishbone diagram, 54
 five-why analyses, process 5, 55
 five-why analysis, process 1, 54–55
 gap visualization, 47–48
 Jishuken (self-learning) activity, 45–46
 kaizen activity, 45
 monitoring results, 58
 normal *vs.* abnormal paint layering, 50
 panel test, 44
 Pareto chart, 48–49
 primer application process, 51–52
 root cause analysis, 54–56
 Scatter plot, 51
 subgroups and examination, 47–53
 sub-KPI vs. main KPI targets, 53
 visual defects, 44
Pareto chart, 48–49
Problem solving, 14–16, 20, 30, 44–46
 8-step problem-solving, 46, 61
 differences in TPS, 60–62
 five-why analyses, in jishuken, 54, 55
 management principles, 43
  measurement, 43
  standardization, 43
  measurement, 43
  standardization, 43
 massive vehicle recall, 2010, 31–32
 paint shop process, *see* Paint shop
  process
 root cause problem solving, 31
 Toyota Business Practice, 31

Process cycle time, 105
Pull system, 26–27, 67

Quality gate, 45, 52
Quality improvement framework, 88–90

Respect and humility, 39
Richardson, Tracey, 59
Root cause problem solving, 31, 45, 72,
 91–92

Safe process design, 28–29
Safety process design, 28
Sakichi Toyoda, 18, 24, 30–31
 early life, 24
 jidoka device, 24
 study methods, 24, 29
Scatter plot, 51
Shook, John, 59
Socratic coaching method, 4, 6, 13
Spirituality, 18–19, 41, 101
 practices, 41
Stability, 23
Standardization, 4, 28, 30, 37–38, 43, 69,
 71, 87
Standardized work, 4
 charts and tools, 4–5, 13
 definition, 2
 kaizen training, *see* Kaizen training
 training practices, 7–8
 try-on-own approach, 11
Standardized work chart, 106–107
for moving line, 108
Standardized work combination table,
 105–106
Supplier Commodity Engineering (SCE), 34

Takt time, 26
TBP, *see* Toyota Business Practice (TBP)
Team work thinking, 38
Time measurement sheet, 103–105
Total productive maintenance (TPM), 23
Toyoda, Akio, 32
Toyoda Kiichiro, 25
Toyota Business Practice (TBP), 31
Toyota Engagement Equation
 (Richardson), 59

118 ■ *Index*

Toyota Motor Company in Japan (TMC-Japan), 33–34
Toyota Motor Manufacturing, Kentucky (TMMK), 7
  production team experience, 7–8
  standardized work trials, 11
Toyota Production System Support Center (TSSC), 62, 90
Toyota Production System (TPS), 1, 7, 20, 21, 45, 62
  academic background, 5
  coaching style, 3, 12–13, 19
  culture, *see* Toyota Production System (TPS)
  discipline, 2
  humility, 15
  problem-solving, 72
  pull system, 67
  standardization, 28
  standardized work training, 2
  TPS values transfer, 15
Toyota Supplier Support Center (TSSC), 34
TPM, *see* Total productive maintenance (TPM)
TPS, *see* Toyota Production System (TPS)
TPS house, 27

heijunka, 27
jidoka, 22
just-in-time, 22, 25
muda, 23
stability, 23
TPS thinking way and cultural transfusion (TEMA), 33
Training methods, 9
  kaizen training, 2
Training Within Industry (TWI), 8–10
Transformation model, 16, 101–102
  social systems, 17
  spirituality and mindset, 18–19
  technical systems, 16
Transformation stages, Kubler-Ross, 40
True North, 19, 23–24, 26, 43

Unused, 11
U.S. healthcare system, 78

Vehicle paint, 43

Work balance chart, 110–112

Yokoten, 12, 59, 96–99

9781032881157